Evacuee
Behind the Lines
of a Firestorm

Evacuee
Behind the Lines
of a Firestorm

J. S. Cooper

SECRETCOMPASS

Evacuee: Behind the Lines of a Firestorm

published by
Secret Compass
PO Box 1731
Fort Collins, CO 80524

www.evacueebook.com
www.facebook.com/evacueebook

print ISBN: 978-0-9895897-0-3
Kindle ISBN: 978-0-9895897-1-0

Cover Photo by Doug Conarroe
Author Photo by Darren Mahuron, Summit Studios
Interior Photos by J. S. Cooper
Cover design by LaVonne Ewing
Text Design by Diane Streb
Edited by Mira Perrizo and Eric Grosshans

Printed in the United States of America

Contents

Preface

To understand this story and the trauma within these pages, one has to understand the enormous amount of energy and determination poured into what was acquired, and what was built. It was a long, long road, simply getting to the beloved valley we would name Ohana, particularly for me.

Anyone who knows me knows that I dreamt of a place like this when I was a young man. Anyone who knows me also knows how hard I worked over the past fifteen years to make that dream a reality.

Now, I'm not pretentious enough to imagine that every person who turns to the first page of this book is going to be interested in these twists and turns along the way, so for those of you that want to get straight to the action, you may want to skip ahead to chapter three. The first two chapters in this story are the pathway to Ohana, and how it came to be...

ONE

Foundation

I grew up in Kaiserslautern, Germany—"K-Town" for short. My parents worked for DoDDS (Department of Defense Dependent Schools), a government program that provides the U.S. military bases overseas with schools and teachers.

We lived in a small German village and I spent my early years playing with the local kids, immersed in the German way of life. My upbringing consisted of a partial exposure to American culture as seen on the U.S. military bases where I went to school, set to a European backdrop. My friends and I all got into skateboards and music at an early age, and by the time we all had cars, everyone was either in bands or preoccupied with going to see bands play.

I graduated from Kaiserslautern American High School in 1989 and ended up at the University of West Florida in Pensacola, Florida. I had a difficult time adjusting to life in the U.S., particularly life in the South, and was in and out of trouble. I did manage to finish with a Bachelor of Science Degree in Industrial Technology/Building Construction at the end of 1993, but for all general purposes, despite the friends I made along the way, my time in the U. S. had not done me well.

After I received my diploma, I immediately returned to K-Town and plunged back into music full time. My friend Allen was putting a lot of energy into a new project that had developed in my absence, a project that fused electronica and heavy guitars together, and he was looking for another vocalist to launch the live shows. It was my first serious shot at becoming a vocalist and I didn't need to be asked twice.

It all began in late 1993 with a single studio microphone and the two of us screaming into it. As dual MCs for HeadCrash we would go on to spend the next six years writing lyrics, making and selling 100,000-plus records for two major labels, touring more than a dozen countries, annihilating some of the biggest forums/stages across Europe and the U.S., and raging late into the night like there was no tomorrow. HeadCrash gave birth to half a dozen additional music projects along the way, not to mention countless friends and mind-blowing experiences that I will never forget as long as I live. It was the thrill ride of a lifetime, packed into just a few short years.

More than anything, I learned a lot about what it took to front a band, what it took to be a leader, and what it meant to have vision. HeadCrash gave me a small taste of success at an early age, and unknowingly, the virtues I would need to try and succeed later in life. Ambition and hard work will eventually pay off, especially if you have the determination and the vision to see a new idea develop until it takes hold.

Unfortunately for me, I would not realize any of this any time soon. Shortly into the pre-production of the second record for the deal we had signed with Sony Music, HeadCrash parted ways with Sony. The band spiraled into a maelstrom of disarray, driven by miscommunication and musical /philosophical differences that ultimately led to the band's demise at the end of April, 1999. In the end, I was stealing food to eat and I was suicidal. I wish that didn't sound so dismal, but it's the truth. To make a long story short, I made the decision to walk away from everything I knew and everything I loved, into the unknown. It was one of the hardest decisions I have ever had to make, but somehow I found the strength to see myself through the pain and heartache to a new life. With tears streaming down my face, I boarded a one-way flight out of Germany.

I spent the next couple of months in seclusion, living with my dad in the mountains of Idaho, north of Spokane, Washington. The time I spent there did me good; it gave me time to gain some perspective as I thought about what I wanted to do with the rest of my life.

I quickly came to the realization that I wasn't going to stay in an economically depressed area of the country and waste away in one of the local saw mills for six dollars an hour so with that in mind, sometime in July of that year, I packed my clothes and my CDs into a car and headed south for Colorado. I had visited a few friends who lived there in the mid 1990s and had often thought about moving there.

I ended up in Denver for the first seven or eight months working different jobs, but I wasn't really happy living paycheck to paycheck and I wasn't happy living in such a big city. I found myself in Fort Collins every weekend, a college town about an hour north of Denver.

Fort Collins is nestled right against the mountains and that meant adventure, in the company of people that also sought adventure. Plus, I had a couple of old friends from K-Town that lived there, so in May of 2000, I relocated. I had visited Fort Collins for the first time in 1994, and somehow I knew I'd be living there some day. It took me five years to realize that this would be my destiny.

I spent the next year and a half at the only job I could find in Fort Collins—on the floor of one of the local warehouses, picking and packing orders. The company was lackluster about recognizing hard work and stingy with the raises, so I was still broke all the time. I shared one side of a duplex with two room-mates and brown-bagged it to work to make ends meet.

Nevertheless, I kept handing out résumés until I got my first real opportunity in August of 2001, testing software for a company that had a contract with Hewlett Packard. My friend's mom was the manager of the project so it appeared that I would get the job before I ever set foot in the building, but I still took the interview seriously and put on a suit and tie. It was a glorious moment when I received the phone call telling me I had gotten the job.

My life changed, seemingly overnight. My pay nearly doubled, which gave me the first taste of having a little bit of freedom. For the first time in years, it seemed, I had a little money to buy the things I wanted and to go out to eat once in a while. The new job also got me into the company of people who were really intelligent, and that meant I'd be learning a lot. I was thrilled to be on board.

My team was testing the software behind CD and DVD writers, in a variety of languages, on a variety of operating systems. In a short amount of time, I learned how to run computers, but more importantly, how to use them as tools to hatch new ideas.

It was somewhere in my spare time working for Hewlett

Packard that I discovered online auctions, the gateway to my own future. You could sell just about anything to just about anyone, just about anywhere in the world. I couldn't believe that such a thing existed. I initially started off as a buyer, and after researching as much as I could on how it all worked, I began to sell.

I quickly realized a formula by which to operate: buy in small markets and sell in big markets. There are lots of people applying this strategy every day now, around the U.S. and abroad. For example: if you buy goods at yard sales, thrift stores, or on Craigslist (small market) and then advertise online (big market), you'll find a lot more buyers and be able to charge more for the same goods.

As I type this, there are people around the world who are rummaging through racks of used clothes and shelves full of antiques, hoping to find a good deal locally on something they can turn around and sell online for a profit. I certainly didn't invent this concept of buying in small markets and selling in big markets, that's for sure, but I definitely put it to work in my own way.

I began to dig up sources for rare music and film in far away places; I would buy hard-to-find titles in bulk and then resell individually to buyers who didn't know where to look. This expanded into a number of new ideas, including a mail order catalogue that some friends and I put together to advertise hard-to-find CDs and DVDs. I titled it "Lifeboat," after the last HeadCrash record we did for Sony Music. It wasn't very lucrative, but it put a little extra money in my pocket so it was worth the time.

Aside from that, I was really happy to be working for a decent wage and really happy to be in the company of people who had ideas. Little did I know how much happier I would get. I had only been on the job with Hewlett Packard for a few months when one night at a local bar, a co-worker introduced me to a friend of

hers. Her name was Rachel. The micron and the nanosecond...
how delicately they mold fate.

Rachel and I became a couple in a matter of weeks. We
realized after our first date that we lived only three houses away
from each other. She owned a house a little farther up from the
road from where I lived and getting together with her was one
of the easiest things that ever happened to me.

A month into our relationship, I had all four of my wisdom
teeth pulled and she took care of me like we had been together
for years. I knew I was in love. We happily spent the next six
months reconsidering our lives as we pondered a future together.

The following summer, the decision was made to renovate
Rachel's old garage into an art studio. David, Rachel's father, is
a prominent attorney in Fort Collins who also has a lot of hands-
on experience in framing and construction. He offered to lead
the way as the foreman, and to lay out in advance the money we
would need to complete the project. We were really grateful to
have his help, but at the same time, this was game-changer for me
as a young man looking to the future. My girlfriend's father had
to pay our way because I didn't have the money, plain and simple.

I'm half Italian, and this is a major no-no in our culture. I
had a choice to make, right then and there. I would either start
getting serious about life and start recognizing the financial reality
of what was coming, or I would keep partying with my friends
and then have to put my hand out to my lady's dad every time
we needed something. Rachel was a total catch, and I felt that
I had to start paying serious attention to the nest if I wanted to
keep her. I don't mean to make this sound so heavy, but looking
back on it all, this was a major crossroads for me.

Fortunately for everyone involved, including myself, I made
the right decision and got serious about the future. I worked over-

time at my job any time it was offered, and every spare moment past that went into expanding the CD and DVD catalogue. After dating for about a year, I moved in with Rachel and started financing various upgrades to the house with what little money I had managed to accumulate. Every spare penny went into renovating our home. We were always busy with projects in those early years and time flew by.

It was sometime that autumn that something amazing happened to me, just by chance. It would change my life as I knew it, and I didn't even see it coming. That autumn, I walked into Best Buy and bought *The Lord of the Rings: The Two Towers* on DVD. It was the Extended Version DVD box set and it came with these two little bookends made from polystone. The attention to detail on these bookends took me by surprise. They were marketed by a company out of California called Sideshow Collectibles, a company I had never heard of.

I got online and checked out their website. The bookends were just the tip of the iceberg. This company was marketing all kinds of comic book and movie-related figures. Basically, they had invested in the idea that people who had collected plastic action figures as kids might be interested in nicer figures with far more detail as adults.

I began buying as a fan at full retail because I really liked the merchandise. It didn't take long for the little light bulb to go on over my head. The thinking was small at first…*If I buy four, and sell three, I'll make enough to cover the one I want to keep for myself.* Then I began to wonder if we could add the figures to the CD and DVD mail order catalogue. The thinking quickly expanded…*If I can buy ten at a reduced price, then I can make something on each one, and make a little money to help with the bills.*

I contacted Sideshow and inquired about a wholesale discount for bulk purchasing. They did in fact have a dealer program and my mail order catalogue qualified for a wholesale account. I immediately began to list the figures in the catalogue and on various auction platforms online.

Over the next few months, I came across other small companies that were manufacturing similar figures and other movie-related merchandise, and I was able to come to terms with those companies as well. In time, I had arranged for wholesale accounts with most of the manufacturers in the fledgling limited edition collectibles world.

The Lifeboat mail order catalogue became Secret Compass in 2003. It was the beginning of a new chapter in my life and I was determined to make something of it. As with any start-up business, though, I didn't really make any money in those first couple of years. No one had ever heard of Secret Compass and prospective buyers were reluctant to trust a company that they had never heard of. I couldn't seem to turn a profit. Plus, I was new to the game, so I made a lot of mistakes and lost money.

I would have been justified in throwing in the towel on my new idea numerous times along the way, but I didn't. I look back to the time I spent with HeadCrash and I'm thankful of what I learned in those years. I'm really grateful I didn't turn my back on Secret Compass. It would prove to be one of the smartest decisions I ever made.

* * *

The years began to blur together, as they do when you're busy and you're having fun. Rachel and I continued to make improvements to our house and in between the various art and music projects we both had going, I finally popped the big question.

I won't get into the details of those precious few seconds,

which took nine months of planning to get to, but thankfully she said yes. We got married shortly thereafter, in June of 2004. It was a grand celebration that brought both of our families and most of our friends together.

Sometime later that summer, Rachel's father and I began to discuss the idea of a "family campus." It was just an idea…what if we could find a piece of land somewhere off the beaten path and build a few houses? The idea of Rachel and I raising our family in a place where our parents could be part of our daily lives was wildly appealing to me. It tied so many of my philosophies in life together.

For starters, getting out of the city and into nature was something I had talked about since I was in high school. As an angry young man, I raved about building a "compound surrounded by concertina wire, guard towers, and a moat filled with alligators! Diesel! Cyanide!"

Obviously, all of that sounds paranoid and crazy to me nowadays, but the basic principle of it never changed, despite all the years that have passed and the changes I've gone through. The idea of "let's get out of town and put our hands into the soil" was never far from my thoughts. This was not a new revelation to me.

Furthermore, I have always felt a sense of obligation toward my parents and the generations that came before me. As a matter of respect, I have always had great disdain for the "out with the old, in with the new" machinery of our age. *Gimme a Pepsi and get out of my way, old man.* How and when did we come to such a complete disregard for our seniors—people that worked their whole lives and would like to finish out their years with some dignity?

It'll be a cold day in hell before I ever put either of my parents into a nursing home and I remember telling both of them that at an early age. I'll work until my hands bleed and I'll share my last piece of bread to make sure that never happens.

I honestly don't believe that human beings were ever meant to live in these compartmentalized boxes, separated from one another physically and emotionally. People have lived in extended groups since the dawn of humanity; this whole idea that we should be split up like we have been in the last hundred years seems to have backfired.

I happen to think that many of the chronic problems in modern society can be traced to the lack of family structure and the support system that comes with it. I don't know how we came to condemning our parents to finish their lives separated from their children and their grandchildren. They took care of us when we were too weak to take care of ourselves, can we not do the same for them in their time of need? The extended family, the community, the tribe, the young learning from the old—isn't that how it's supposed to be?

I happen to agree, so when David and I began to explore the outskirts of Fort Collins for possible locations for this family campus, I put real time and energy into it. The first few locations we scouted had glaring problems and one by one, we crossed them off the list. They were either too small, too expensive, or had too many restrictions. I would come to realize in the years ahead that society is no longer structured to accommodate the extended family, and it's an uphill battle to try and get anyone in power to have any vision.

Restriction is in everything from the financial institutions that call the shots to land-use and the municipalities that control it. One residence per parcel of land and anything more than that calls for special hearings to try and change the system.

We had all but given up hope on finding the right piece of

land when, in November of 2004, Rachel's brother stumbled upon a listing that had just come onto the market. Tomas was a real estate agent at the time and he was also keen to see the "family campus" become a reality. I'll never forget the first day we all drove out to see it for the first time. "Wilderness Ranch," a sixty-five-acre parcel of land up Buckhorn Canyon—five cabins, two barns, and various other outbuildings. The sixty-five acres covered a whole mountain and a lush valley below it that was filled with dense foliage and broadleaf cottonwoods. There was a stream running through the valley and it fed a lake that was three acres in size and twelve feet deep.

The sun shone down upon us as our family walked the land together for the first time. I felt like I was in paradise. I knew right then and there that I would do everything in my power to make the dream a reality.

At the time, Wilderness Ranch was owned by a lady by the name of Jan, who was using the land and the barns as a sanctuary for abused farm animals. Believe it or not, some people do unspeakable things to their own animals in the course of running agricultural businesses.

Jan would go in and rescue cows, chickens, pigs, turkeys, and other animals from various farms in the area, some of them left for dead. She would offer room and board in the various cabins on the property to anyone that volunteered to help.

Her heart was in the right place, but after accumulating literally hundreds of animals over the twelve-year period that she owned the ranch, she came to the end of the line. No one really knew if it was the overwhelming amount of work, the lack of funding to keep it all going, or something else that brought her to the decision to call it quits and put the property up for sale.

I don't think we were the first prospective buyers to show any interest in Wilderness Ranch, but I do think she was impressed with our idea to make the ranch into a family campus, if we could come up with the funding to acquire it. Her support would make the all difference in the months ahead.

Shortly after our trip up Buckhorn Canyon, our extended family embarked on a three-week excursion to New Zealand. The trip was originally planned as just a vacation, but due to the recent developments, the trip came to be something more than just a family outing.

Rachel and I, along with her parents and her brother and his family—these would be the three households that would try and pool their money together to acquire Wilderness Ranch in the new year, and the trip actually became somewhat of a test for all of us—Rachel, Shane, David, Lisa, Tomas, Karen, and their four-year-old son, Jack.

Could we all get along? Could we all get along well enough to sell our homes and commit to moving forty-five minutes away from civilization, into the wilderness, together? Would we be willing to blur the lines between our incomes and our needs as individuals and as couples to seek something greater than our compartmentalized boxes in town?

It all came down to the trip to New Zealand and what the trip would tell us about each other. To summarize, it couldn't have gone better. The seven of us spent the next three weeks on the open road together, traveling in a rented camper and a second vehicle. We planned meals, ate together, and slept in the camper plus one small tent. We trekked through the majority of the cities and the countryside of New Zealand, and we did it as a family.

Now, I'm not going to pretend that we got along every second of every day and I'm also not going to pretend that we could've all moved into one big house together like the Brady Bunch.

Realistically, the idea of a family campus came with natural boundaries that were pretty clear to everyone involved. We were all going to have our own homes and our own autonomy. Rachel and I weren't ever going to be sharing a fridge with her parents, and her parents weren't ever going to be coming downstairs to tell us to "keep it down" if we had friends over. All of this was established well in advance, with almost no discussion. It was just a given. Naturally, there were differences of opinion as the days came and went on our trip together, but it was clear that everyone involved was willing to compromise, and that was a clear reflection of what the future would look like. There was a level of mutual respect for one another and that made for a strong foundation. I can honestly say that I came back from the trip feeling more convinced than ever that the move to acquire Wilderness Ranch as a family was to be our destiny.

As crazy as it sounds, the decision to move forward on the family campus at the beginning of 2005 was actually the easy part. Tomas and Karen put their house in town on the market, as did David and Lisa. Rachel and I decided that we would rent out our house when we vacated it.

Everyone was in agreement; we would collectively try to qualify for the funding we would need to acquire Wilderness Ranch and then vacate the homes we had in town if we succeeded.

Like I said, this was the easy part. Convincing any one of the financial institutions on Earth to lend us the money was the hard part. Despite the fact that we had the down payment they required, had good credit scores, and collectively met the minimum income requirements to move forward with the financing, none of the banks would budge.

They were skeptical of everything, including the cash in our bank accounts. I was told that my funds weren't "seasoned,"

which in short meant that my money hadn't sat long enough
in my account to be taken seriously. I remember bellowing into
the phone on more than one occasion. It was a really frustrating
experience that dragged on for weeks, and then months.

We began to look into alternatives, including trying to raise
private funding through members of our families and selling off
assets. Nothing materialized. Just when we were about to give up
all hope, Tomas and David came up with a brilliant plan.

The banks didn't seem to want to lend us the money to initially acquire the ranch, but if we were able to somehow acquire
it on our own, even temporarily, the policies that applied to *refinancing* property already in our possession were far more flexible.

The trick of it was to somehow get the ranch legally into our
names so that the banks would bite on the refinancing part of
it. We approached Jan with our idea…if she would take the 10
percent down payment we had and "carry" the sale, meaning
that if she would sell to us without us having all the money up
front, we could turn around and get the rest of the money once
we refinanced the property.

After reviewing the documents, Jan accepted the proposal
and Wilderness Ranch was legally sold to David. The ink was
barely dry on the signatures when we turned around and refinanced the property with one of the local banks. Within a couple
months, Jan got the rest of her money and at last Wilderness
Ranch was ours.

We had a 52-foot trailer hauled to the property to store our
furniture and on a day at the end of April, 2005, in the middle
of a snowstorm, we moved three families and their households
into the five cabins on our new family campus. At the end of the
day we were exhausted, but very, very happy.

Little did we know how many times in a single week we'd

experience this same exhaustion in the years ahead. Little did we know how much stress and frustration we would endure to achieve our goals in the years ahead. I look back on it all and I can't believe what we accomplished in the face of the adversity we experienced.

It was the beginning of an adventure, filled with extreme highs and lows, and to sit where I'm sitting right now, I'm 100 percent certain that we made the right decision when we sold our homes and left town.

TWO

In the Thick of It

The first two weeks were really hard, I have to admit it. The cabin that Rachel and I moved into was in bad shape. It had literally been condemned when we had the property inspected as part of the acquisition. The county inspectors looked us right in our faces and told us, "Don't let anybody live in there." There we were, three or four days into it, sitting in a dilapidated, condemned cabin in the middle of nowhere, shivering.

It was heated with a thirty-year-old propane stove that made the hallway it sat in toasty warm, but left the rest of the cabin uncomfortably cold. The roof leaked and the walls weren't insulated. The floors didn't have any insulation beneath them either, and it was unbearable to walk around without at least one pair of socks on.

The pipes behind the kitchen sink froze any time the temperature dipped into the single digits. The living room had absolutely no source of heat in it, so you either chopped wood and kept the fireplace going, or you froze. The cabin was also filled with mice that we couldn't keep out no matter how hard we tried.

On top of that, I had moved Secret Compass into a two-car garage on Mason Street when we left Fort Collins and that garage didn't have an adequate heat source in it either. Between the cabin and the garage, I just couldn't seem to get warm and the forty-five-minute commute I had for my day job with Hewlett Packard wasn't making me feel any better about our new life.

We had just finished the renovations on our house in town when we moved out of it, and because we didn't even get a chance to enjoy what we had worked so hard to complete, we felt like we had missed out on something. The hardships we faced in the cabin made us miss our house in town that much more.

I can honestly say that in the first few months of living on the ranch, I secretly wondered if we had made the wrong move, or if we were crazy, or both. It was more than the first few months—it was that whole first year. I quickly came to realize that we didn't know anything about living in the country. We didn't know where the wells were that pumped our water, and once we figured that out, we weren't sure how the plumbing was routed to the individual cabins.

Furthermore, we didn't even know where to begin when it came to maintaining the property. Around fifteen of the sixty-five acres are pastures and that has to be mowed as soon as the grass starts to grow or it's a lost cause. Once the grass is more than a foot high, snakes get in there and then you can't even walk in it without risking getting bitten. We realized this all too late that first summer, and by the time we bought a riding mower, the pastures were too far gone.

If I remember right, we ended up hiring someone for $45 an hour, a "fire prevention and mitigation expert." The guy shows up with a couple of weed eaters and a bunch of syllables woven into his job title and that commanded $45 an hour. I just shook my head as he pranced around with his weed eater. We had a lot to learn.

The situation with the farm animals also complicated life on the ranch in that first year. Jan had tried to find alternate homes for all the animals that had come to the ranch before she left, but in the end she did leave us with a few pigs, a few sheep, some chickens, and a couple of turkeys.

We cared for them as part of our new life on the ranch, but then when one of the sheep went down for the count and we had to rush it to the vet, we realized that we didn't know anything about caring for farm animals. Four hundred dollars later, we came to the conclusion that the remaining animals on the ranch would be better off in care of another animal sanctuary and we were fortunate enough to find one close to Fort Collins. They came and took the remaining animals.

In the course of cleaning out the barns, we came upon maintenance project after maintenance project, many of which required immediate attention. It was pretty clear that Jan's funding had dried up long ago, and the condition of the grounds we had inherited was proof positive. Everything seemed to be held together by caulk and bailing wire.

There were miles and miles of fencing that had been used to keep the animals separated from each other that was cobbled together with everything from nails and chicken wire to screws and bungee cords. David, Tomas, and I spent that entire first summer tearing the fences down. Occasionally, we had a tractor on loan from one of David's clients, but for the most part it was manual labor and brute force. We went to sleep utterly exhausted on multiple nights of the week.

Despite our jagged adaptation to country life in that first year, there was a lot to be happy about. We were all in it together, for starters. That meant a lot of laughs, campfires, great meals, and cold beers in each other's company, including the company of our friends and other family members that frequently came to visit. The first garden we grew that year was a major success and we ate from it like kings and queens when it was time to harvest. I couldn't believe how much work we were able to get done when we all worked together. There were tasks that used to take Rachel and me all weekend to finish in our garden back in Fort Collins, that only took a few hours to accomplish—with six sets of hands working the soil instead of two. We were seeing strength in numbers, in real time. It was amazing.

Better yet, it was so much more fun to work together with my extended family than by myself. We were collectively left with an enormous sense of pride at the end of the day, admiring what we had just fixed or created.

As summer became autumn, I convinced my dad to sell his place in Idaho and move to Colorado to be with us. His relocation happened in a matter of only one or two months, as he already had a buyer lined up. We had another trailer hauled in and the movers transferred all of his household goods into it, to be stored until we built new homes.

All of a sudden, my dad was a permanent resident at the ranch and for the first time since I had left for college, there would be no more goodbyes. I'm sitting here thinking of all the train stations and airports we had to part ways in over the years and it brings tears to my eyes knowing that he is here on the ranch with me and I can look after him for the rest of his life. Great, now I'm crying.

Okay, before I proceed…one thing that deserves mentioning.

We both knew in 2005 that it made all the sense in the world for him to move to Colorado to be with me, but at the end of the day I still think it took a lot of courage for him to leave the tranquility of his home in Idaho overlooking Mt. Spokane to come live in a thirty-year-old camper parked next to our dilapidated cabin, with a bunch of other people he barely knew. That takes vision and I'm proud of my dad for making the jump.

If I remember right, he arrived just in time for Thanksgiving that year. It was an Epic Fail Thanksgiving, who could forget… Tomas attempted to deep-fry a turkey in a vat of oil. He was smart enough to keep the whole operation far away from his house, so he wasn't one of those idiots you see on the news every year that burns their house down on Thanksgiving attempting to do the same thing, but he did manage to turn one fine turkey into a fifteen-pound lump of coal.

He realized thirty to forty minutes into the fry that the thermometer he was using was defective, so after turning the propane burner to the highest setting and letting it go for an extended period of time, he completely vulcanized the main course. It was absolutely a solid chunk of nuclear waste. We laughed until it hurt.

I think the vulcanized turkey was the final straw in all of us collectively getting the "Horse's Ass Award" that year. This is a family tradition that goes back twenty-five years; it's given out annually on Christmas Day to the person with the most notable gaffe of the year. The award usually comes with a poem and/ or props and is delivered by the defending champion from the year before.

Normally, the Horse's Ass Award goes to a single individual, but considering how many blunders our extended family had made in our first year at the ranch, Tomas's nuclear turkey included, the award was given to *all* of us that year. I believe it was David that sheepishly accepted it on behalf of everyone as the rest of us heehawed our way through our first Christmas in Buckhorn Canyon.

All in all, despite the difficulties in adapting to country life and all the setbacks we experienced with the property, the animals, and the structures, no one had moved back to town and this was invigorating—to everyone involved.

Amidst everything that happened in that first year, the last sign for Wilderness Ranch came off the large barn and we christened our new campus "Ohana," which means family in Hawaiian. I couldn't have imagined a better name.

* * *

We began 2006 with the development of what would become our family garden. It was sometime in February or March of that year that we finally turned our full attention to the field in between the two barns in the valley, an area we had been eyeing for more than a year.

The pig waste left in this field was more than a foot deep in some places and the soil was so "hot" that the weeds wouldn't even grow, but as time would tell, this fertilizer would prove to be worth its weight in gold once it got worked into the soil. After turning it over often in the previous year, we were finally ready to make this field the site of the future Ohana garden.

Lisa and her sister, Laura, who had just moved into one of the cabins on the ranch, put together a loose plan of where we would plant crops, flowers, and herbs. David and I were in charge of the three-zone sprinkler system that would run beneath the garden.

We rented a "ditch witch" from a local tool yard to help us get the job done. This is a machine that will dig ditches, and David and I made the grand mistake of renting the one that you push instead of spending a little more on the bigger one that you ride. Sweet Mother of God.

As we would quickly come to recognize, and I do mean quickly...they don't call it the Rocky Mountains for nothing. The river rock that we began to churn up made it clear that Buckhorn Creek, which was more than two hundred feet away, had at one time flowed through this field. David and I took punishment like you wouldn't believe over the next two days as we pulled thousands of stones out of the ground.

The ditch witch pounded the living daylights right out of us. I would still have the shakes long after we had turned off the damn thing at night. We couldn't get six inches without a fight and some of the rocks were so big that we had to use rail yard crowbars to get them out.

In the end, with Tomas's help, we eventually cleared out all of the ditches to make way for what would be a massive sprinkler system beneath this field. The new garden began that year with a short pathway between two sets of retaining timbers and two small herb crops on either side. It would eventually grow over the years to the very edges of this field.

The year 2006 saw many additional changes, as we slowly began to plan the future of Ohana and the permanent residences that would need to be built. For the purposes of obtaining construction loans and permanent financing on the new houses we wanted to build, we knew we needed to divide Ohana into smaller parcels of land. We weren't really interested in drawing lines in the sand, but we knew that at least symbolically, the lines had to be drawn in order to satisfy building codes and to qualify for loans.

In the opening discussions with Larimer County, we realized early on that it would be a fight and a long one at that. For start-

ers, they weren't going to let us divide the property the way we
wanted to divide it. The original plan we developed in late 2004
called for what's known as a "minor land division," which is the
simplest way to split a single piece of property into smaller parcels.
Normally, in rural Larimer County, the rules state that you
can only have one residence per thirty-five acres, but it had been
intimated to us in the acquisition of the ranch that since there
were already five cabins on the property, these five structures
would be grandfathered in as residences and therefore we would
be able to split Ohana into five unique parcels of land.

The plan all along called for five parcels: David and Lisa
would get one, Tomas and his family would get one, Rachel and
I would get one, my dad would get one, and the last one with the
large barn on it would be shared by all of us, to be remodeled as
a future site for a possible event center.

This was the plan from the very beginning, so that we would
be able to qualify for loans to build new houses and be able to renovate the large barn one day. Larimer County threw that plan into
a complete state of upheaval when they declared that they didn't
consider most of the cabins on the property to be residences.

They informed us that they would only let us divide the property into two parcels. There would be no way we could build our
homes under this proposal. It would be the first of two major
fights and this one lasted about six months.

We immediately went to work on an alternate plan. If I
remember right, there was a big push to acquire five more acres
from one of the neighbors that had land bordering Ohana. This
would bring us from sixty-five to the magical number of seventy
total acres, which would then allow us to divide the property into
two halves, and then divide one of the halves into two pieces.

That would give us at least three unique parcels of land,

but the problem was, none of our neighbors would agree to sell us five of their acres. We tried a "we'll give you cash, and you can still use the five acres as you please" angle, as well as "let us temporarily redraw the lines, then we'll give you back your land after we do our divisions," but no one budged.

Our neighbors were either not willing to sell or too skeptical of our intentions, and we were back to square one. In the end, after an exhaustive bit of research and a couple of affidavits, we were able to prove through old utility bills that one of the cabins that Larimer County had declared "wasn't ever a residence" had in fact been an independent residence for many years.

The county finally relented and that brought us to a point where we would be able divide Ohana into three unique parcels of land. We went back to the drawing board and after reading extensively through the various building codes, we came up with an innovative new plan that would allow us to build all our homes under these limitations.

David and Lisa would get the piece of the property with the large barn and two of the cabins on it, Tomas and his family would get another piece of the property with two cabins on it, and Rachel, my dad, and I would get the last piece of property with the cabin we were living in.

In order to be able to renovate the large barn at a later date, David and Lisa came up with tentative plans to physically connect their future home to the barn via the roofline—creating a "breezeway." That meant that the two structures would actually be viewed as one, and thus easier to deal with regarding permits.

In order to build two new houses on the single piece of the property Rachel and I would share with my dad, we had a couple of options. The first choice was set up by Larimer County specifically to "care for the elderly."

You could build a new house and also have a separate residence for whoever was elderly, but that second residence couldn't be a "permanent residence," and you had to get the permit renewed every two years, and that second residence had to be physically removed from the property once the elderly person was no longer there.

Basically, that meant my dad could haul in and live in a trailer or manufactured home and hope to get the permit renewed every two years. *He's not dead yet? Okay here's another signature. Make sure you check back in two years.* It was an insulting proposition, to say the least.

There was no way on Earth I was going to put my dad through that, not after all the sacrifices he made for our family all those years. Not a chance in hell. Option #1 was off the table without ever getting onto the table. We had to come up with something crafty, and that we did—Option #2.

It was a relatively new code that had only come about in the last few years. You could build what was known as a "primary residence" and then also build a secondary structure, a "detached garage with accessory living quarters," both on a single piece of property. There were all kinds of limitations to it, but we eventually came up with a way to make it work.

The secondary structure's square footage could only be 40 percent of the primary structure's square footage, or 800 square feet of livable space, whichever was *less*. This meant that at the most, if Rachel and I built a house with at least 2,000 square feet of livable space, my dad could only get a maximum of 800 square feet in his house. Excuse me, "detached garage with accessory living quarters." God forbid I would call my dad's house an actual house around anyone official in the months ahead.

My dad freaked out at first because he had just sold his 1,800 square foot home plus a two-car garage up in Idaho before moving to Colorado. Even with some downsizing, he wasn't happy about squeezing his life into 800 square feet.

We were so pissed off at the parameters of the situation that we didn't catch the fine print. It would take two or three days of lamenting about the county and their endless regulations before we re-read the code and found a loophole—800 square feet of *livable* space. A basement wasn't considered to be livable space, and that meant that my dad could build 800 square feet on top of 800 square feet. All of a sudden, my dad had the possibility of building a 1,600-square-foot structure and still be within the code.

Provided, of course, that we held public meetings, got permission from all our neighbors, and scheduled a special hearing with Larimer County. Not to mention getting signatures from the county's Engineering and Planning Division, as well as the Water Division. It was a daunting uphill battle with a rusty musket, and it had just begun.

The second major fight between Ohana and Larimer County came about when we applied for the "minor land division" to divide the ranch into three pieces. Engineering and Planning basically told David to his face that we'd be giving them free land or he wouldn't get the signature he needed to complete the division. David's initial answer was "not only no, but hell no."

We initially thought we had grounds to take the county to court for attempting to extort us, but the more we looked into it, the more we realized that we were screwed. To summarize, this has to do with "eminent domain" and the underhanded new way of twisting it.

Eminent domain means that if the city or county wants to build or widen a road, build an aqueduct, or anything like that, they have a right to take private land if it's in the way. They have to pay the landowner current market value for their land, which is nothing new, but there's a new twist.

Here's the trick of it…in order to avoid having to pay for the land they seize when they announce a new project, they try and get it for free, in advance, if you ever happen to need anything from them. In other words, if you need their approval like we needed approval to divide Ohana, guess what? Sign over the land to the county for future use, for free, or no signatures.

They wanted an eight-foot strip of land along the county road that runs by our property in case they ever wanted to widen the road, which amounted to almost three acres of land, for free! Like I said, the initial answer was "HELL NO," but the further we got into researching it, the more we realized how futile it would be to try and sue.

There are municipalities all over the United States that are doing this and getting away with it. It would take years' worth of time and an exorbitant amount of money, even for an attorney such as David, to even see our day in court. What were we supposed to do, sit around cursing the county, with our lives and future plans on pause forever?

In the end, we begrudgingly signed over the land, but with one major stipulation. David knows how to professionally negotiate and he drove a hard bargain. They could take the land, but the fence along the county road, which was now on their newly acquired eight-foot strip of property, would stay where it was until the county had an actual use for the land they took from us.

So basically, after all that, nothing really changed in our lives. Until the county decides to widen the road, which could be a hundred years from now, if at all, our fence stays on their land and that means we can still use the eight-foot strip of land they stole from us. It's fenced into our land until further notice.

With this agreement, we did get the signature we needed from Engineering and Planning, and that left only one thing that stood in the way of us dividing the property and proceeding with our individual plans to build.

The Division of Water demanded that we show that we had sufficient resources to serve the final number of homes that the ranch would have. There are two wells on the property and they were adequately serving everyone that lived there, but that wasn't the kind of hard evidence that the county needed in order to approve our plans.

We contacted the outfit that had serviced the wells before we acquired the ranch. They didn't have any documentation. We contacted the original company that actually bored the second well in 1994, but they didn't have any documentation either.

In a mad dash to recover something, anything that showed that the two wells on the property were adequate for what we wanted to do, we came across a single document from the Division of Water itself, among the papers Jan left us when she sold us the ranch.

It clearly showed that each well had the GPM (gallons per minute) to serve up to three residences, for a total of six. That was more than enough to adequately service what structures were already there when we acquired the ranch, plus what we hoped to build.

It all came down to that single document, sitting in a stack of papers in the back of a closet. I wonder to this day what would have happened if that stack of papers had accidentally been misplaced or thrown out. We were either really lucky or it was just meant to be.

Within a month the surveyors had come and gone, the minor land division was approved, and Ohana was officially divided into three unique plots of land, on paper. That meant that the access driveway that came in from the county road was officially open to public use, and that meant that the county would let us name the driveway. It became "Ohana Way," and I remember grinning from ear to ear the day they showed up to install the official green sign at the entrance to the property.

* * *

Soon after we had completed the minor land division, David and Lisa wasted no time in getting their blueprints and their financing lined up. They would be ready to break ground on their new home at the end of the year. Rachel, my dad, and I were going to need more time. A lot more time.

My dad had made up his mind when he first came to the ranch that he wanted to be on the mountain at the very top of the property. Since there wasn't even a road to get up there, much less electricity or water, I tried to talk him out of it. I didn't think it would be financially possible for him to swing the costs of building a house, plus all the added costs of access and utilities.

Also, Rachel and I weren't initially sure of where we wanted to build. It had to be within the confines of the plot of land that was in our name, that much was certain. I had originally looked into completely renovating and adding onto the cabin we were living in, but given all the problems with the structure, we decided that we would build something new.

We originally considered building in the field behind the cabin, but the massive snowstorm that hit us earlier that winter left more than three feet of snow on the ground and standing water in that field for weeks on end when it melted. I wasn't going to fight the water table for the rest of my life, so that was out.

We considered building right into the mountainside just

above the field; that was also an option. I took a hike one day to check it all out and had an epiphany. Why would we build at the bottom of the mountainside when we could build farther up the mountain and have a nice view of the lake? There was a spot where the land leveled off a bit, and it was right next to where the access road would go if my dad got his wish and built at the top of the mountain like he wanted to.

The final plan came together in a matter of hours, it seemed. Rachel and I would build about half way up the mountain, and my dad would build at the top of the mountain. We would split the costs of an access road that would come in right between our two new houses and also split the costs on bringing in utilities.

I remember the night I ran it all by Rachel; she stared at me like I had just fallen out of a spaceship. Fortunately, I had never completely failed at any of the other crazy ideas I had run by her, so she believed in me enough to let me get started on the bids. It was the beginning of an incredible amount of work that damn near consumed me.

* * *

That summer, we began our bidding process for the new road that would climb the mountain and give us access to the two new building sites. We called up a few excavation companies and had them give us an estimate on what the costs would be. The first company came out and measured, and got back to us with a bid of $10,000.

My dad and I figured that was reasonable, five grand for each building site. We certainly weren't going to get out there with shovels and dig it ourselves. The next company that came along said they'd do it for $7,000. Even better, that was only $3,500 for each site.

I was just about to hire the second company and not bother meeting with a third guy, but then I thought it wouldn't hurt to just wait another day or two. Dan from Kramer Excavation, aka Dan the Digger, showed up a couple of days later.

He got out and surveyed the land and when he was done, we met up at the bottom of the mountain. "I'll do it for three thousand." I kept my composure until he was gone. $3,000???? There had to be something wrong, there was no way this guy could come in at less than a third of another bid, and still give us quality work.

I called him up the next day and asked for references, and then drove out to see other driveways in the area he had cut. They all looked like roads that had been there for centuries. It turned out that Dan the Digger didn't have a big company with a lot of overhead. It was just him and his wife. He had left Fort Collins in the early '70s after hearing one too many sirens go by his house and retreated to a cabin he built himself up in Rist Canyon.

Over the past thirty years, he'd earned a modest reputation in the local area by doing good work, all with his own excavator and his own dump truck. Needless to say, we hired him to cut the new driveway up the mountain and consequently, all the other digging we'd ever need after that. He broke ground on the new road in September of 2006. It took him only three days to finish the job.

In the meantime, shortly after Christmas of that year, the construction crew that David and Lisa hired to build their house broke ground. Their house went up in the spring of 2007, and I think they moved into it that summer. We hoped to be in our new house within a year. That turned out to be wishful thinking. Getting a road to our building site was just the beginning.

The next step was putting in utilities and that proved to be more of a challenge than we expected. It's not like building a house in town where electricity, water, and sewage come right to the edge of the vacant lot you're building on. You just connect to what's already there and presto, your new house has utilities. Building in the country is a whole other story.

First off, Poudre Valley REA (the company that provides electrical service to rural Larimer County) wanted $5,000 to put in the two new power poles we would need to get power up the mountain. Really? *I have to pay you five grand so you can bring service to my house, and then you make money off that service, forever and ever? Seems like a business expense you guys might want to cover yourselves, if you want to make some serious money off a future client?* I didn't get it, but I didn't have a choice. Either come up with the $5,000 or go solar, which I wasn't prepared to pay for at the time.

The two poles would bring electricity to within fifty feet of the place where I wanted to build a home for Rachel and me, but that was still three hundred feet from where my dad wanted to build. Then there was the question of water and phone lines.

In the end, after a lot of planning, we decided that we would need to dig a massive trench from the well at the bottom of the valley all the way to the top of the mountain. It would run water up to the main house half way up the mountain, and then continue with water, electricity, and phone service all the way to my dad's site.

We called up Dan the Digger, who came back with his excavator and did the job in two days. There were parts of the mountain that were so steep that I thought Dan was going to tip over and tumble down the mountain in his machine. I couldn't bear to watch, it was so scary.

I think he asked for $800 when he was done, which was a fraction of what we would have paid if we had hired anyone else. I felt like having a cape made for him, with his name embroidered on the back. Anyway, in the end we had a three-foot wide trench that ran six feet deep, all the way from the valley up to my dad's site.

To try and save money, we bought the electric cable on a spool and decided to lay it ourselves. What a mistake that was. I should have mounted the spool onto an axle and unwound the cable from end to end, but instead I pulled all the cable off the edge of the spool all at once and was then left trying to man-handle an 800 pound bowl of spaghetti that kept trying to coil itself back up.

It damn near drove me insane, especially because the county wanted the entire cable encased in PVC conduit. After wrestling the cable into the trench, I got to work on the conduit. I threaded each ten-foot section of PVC at the top of the mountain, and then lugged each section all the way down from my dad's site to where the power poles came in.

The conduit was an inch or two wider than the cable, but with all the cable's twists and coils, the friction made the thread-ing of each section of conduit beyond difficult. It was a fight every inch of the way. I was exhausted after two sections, with 280 feet to go. I would spend the next three weeks in this ditch, working like a POW.

In the end, I had a water line running up from the well to the main house site, and then water, electricity, and phone running up from the main house site to my dad's site. Both the electric cable and the phone cable were encased in PVC conduit, which was to code, but after all that, when I called the county's electri-cal engineers to have them inspect it, they flunked the whole thing because they said that the conduit had to be "sealed with an adhesive."

That didn't make any sense at all. It still doesn't. The electric cable itself was already sealed and designed to be buried in the ground without any conduit at all; the protective PVC conduit was just code for Colorado, to keep sharp rocks and stones from interfering with the cable. I hadn't bothered to glue the conduit together because it wasn't in the code and it clearly wasn't necessary, but the county didn't see it that way.

In a mad dash to be done with the ditch once and for all, I raced home from work the next day and got it all done in a single night. I pulled all thirty sections of conduit apart by yanking the first one up four to five feet, and the next one a little less, until I had adequate space in between them all to glue them, and then shove them back together one by one.

It took me three hours. I finished late at night, right as a storm rolled in. Somehow, I managed to get a photo of myself in this ditch (see photo 1) just as the clouds let loose. I look like a vagrant.

The next day I called the electrical engineers to have them come out and inspect the ditch. Much to my utter disbelief, they told me they "didn't have the time to make it out there anytime soon" so they just passed it over the phone, without even coming back out to inspect it again. I was happy to have passed, but shocked at the way the whole thing had unfolded.

I had just put an incredible amount of labor into pulling apart and gluing three hundred feet of PVC in a single night after work—labor that was absolutely meaningless in terms of the future integrity of the cable—only to have them pass it without even acknowledging what that entailed?

It was mind-boggling. I might as well have gone out for drinks and had fun with my friends instead of toiling late into the night in that trench. The glue didn't amount to a damn thing and for all they knew, I didn't even do what I claimed over the phone to have done. I couldn't believe it.

In the end, Dan the Digger filled in the trench and the bittersweet saga went down in history as the massive glue job that I didn't need to do, shouldn't have done, and wouldn't have done if I had known that follow-up inspection was just a farce.

* * *

We decided to have an up-and-coming architect out of Utah design both homes. After much deliberation, we moved forward with the plan to build both structures out of SIPs (Structured Insulated Panels), which are prefabricated panels made out of OSB (Oriented Strand Board) and compressed recycled foam. SIP homes are one and a half times as strong as a traditional home made out of 2x4s and they're super-insulated. The walls would be R-40 and the ceilings would be R-50.

We hired an engineer that helped us position the eaves over all the windows on both structures so that we could maximize passive solar gain. That meant that the low arc of the sun in late autumn, winter, and early spring would hit all the southern windows and warm up the houses. Once the sun rose high enough at the end of spring, it would start to hit the eaves over the windows instead of the glass, so the homes would remain cool throughout the summer.

We were ready to break ground just after Thanksgiving of 2007, but the day the concrete guys arrived to start forming up the basement walls, we got whacked with a snowstorm that would go on to screw up the entire schedule. This was the beginning of serious trouble for us—trying to get cement trucks and heavy equipment up the new road to the building sites in the dead of winter.

We ended up having to bring Dan the Digger back in to widen the road because the company that was hired to bring in the cement was concerned that their trucks wouldn't make it. I spent many an evening plowing, shoveling, scraping, and salting that driveway in anticipation of a delivery the following morning. Between the driveway, the trench, the utilities, and the foundation, we ate dirt for more than a year before there was anything to look at.

The houses began to go up in March of 2008. The superintendent that we hired to manage the project was there to manage the foundations and the basic shells, that was it. This is known as a "shell construct." If you want to pay someone to manage the construction of your new home from start to finish and then hand you a set of keys, you'll pay $40,000 to $50,000 just in management fees. We were looking to save money and I figured that if we could manage the subcontractors ourselves after the walls went up, we'd save $35,000 right there.

I presumed that I had learned enough in school and had enough hands-on experience to handle it. The problem was, I didn't have any idea how much stress I was taking on, or how absolutely exhausting it would all be. I can't begin to tell you how eternally tired I was, day in and day out.

I was working four jobs: a full time job testing software up in Cheyenne, a part time job monitoring data storage in Fort Collins, a part time vending route, and Secret Compass. My weekdays were consumed by these four jobs and my evenings and weekends were consumed by the homes. Every spare second and every spare cent went into planning or completing one project or another.

My morning started every day at 4:30 a.m. and I averaged three to four hours of sleep a night, for what ended up being years on end. I would hear the alarm clock ring in the morning and I wanted to bash it to pieces. Looking back on it all, it made sense to try and manage the completion of the homes myself in order to save $35,000, but I didn't know it would take me to the brink of insanity.

I was constantly arguing with people, mostly subcontractors that were trying to take advantage of us. They could tell that my attention was spread too thin and I couldn't watch all of them at once. Plus, with the freak tornado that blew through a neighboring city that summer, I suddenly found myself with a major shortage of labor and materials. Everyone was scrambling to fix or rebuild structures that had suddenly come down.

The metal for our roofs arrived four months late, and I couldn't get a decent electrician on site to save my life. We were really behind schedule and the bank was on my case because of it. I was on the phone more and more at work and consequently, my boss wrote me up for receiving a "personal fax" on company equipment. I was running the risk of losing my job.

In the middle of it all, our family was thrown into foreclosure on some commercial real estate we had all purchased together in 2003. The economy was falling apart and all of our tenants moved out, all at once. That left our family plus two partners trying to keep an $18,000 mortgage afloat in the middle of what would turn out to be the Recession of 2007-2008.

We made the grand mistake of trying to keep it alive while it hemorrhaged, only to abandon it when we were completely depleted. This commercial property was supposed to be our nest egg, something that we could sell one day and use to pay off Ohana; instead, it gobbled up all our savings and left us broke. I personally lost tens of thousands. Not make-believe equity money, but hard-earned, scraped together money.

To top it all off, I went to the doctor after two weeks of intense pain and was diagnosed with a condition that required immediate surgery. I was so busy with my jobs plus the house that I was back at work the very next day after the surgery. I gritted my teeth and pushed on, but the cracks were starting to show. Literally. At one point, while driving home one night, I punched the inside of my windshield so hard that I shattered it.

The stress was eating me alive. I have never been a quitter, but at the same time, I had never been under such pressure. It was just too much. There were times that I felt like I couldn't take it anymore and I wanted to run away. My old life, a new life, I wasn't sure. I was delirious from the overbearing schedule and lack of sleep. I found myself daydreaming about burning down both structures and getting on a plane, destination anywhere-but-here.

I knew that it was all in my head, but nevertheless I felt like I was losing my mind. We were either going to emerge victorious with two houses shining on the hill or go down in flames. I really needed something to reboot my willpower and in late June, I unsuspectingly got what I asked for.

Rachel was pregnant. We were absolutely ecstatic to get this news, especially considering that we had been trying to get pregnant for the past two years and we were already in the opening stages of the expensive medical procedures that couples try when they can't conceive.

It put us in a race against time to get the house done by the time our son Ben arrived, but it was the reboot I needed. I pressed on even harder. Rachel had soldiered in the cabin for the past three years; it was cold and cramped, and I didn't want her to be uncomfortable any longer than she had to be.

Work continued on the houses throughout summer and autumn, into the winter of 2008. It was one fight after another, trying to get the subcontractors to understand the pressure we were under to get it all done. We hired many of our friends to help and together with our family, they put in long hours with us to make the final push.

Then, just as I thought we were getting close to the finish line, I had one of the worst weeks of my life. All in a single week in December of 2008, I lost my main source of income, we failed all the inspections on the house, I broke a $300 window, and I ran over my father-in-law's dog.

The contract in Cheyenne was unexpectedly cancelled and the rest of it came on consecutive days after that. I didn't even want to get out of bed anymore; I was so physically and emotionally exhausted from the long haul and from the mistakes I had made along the way.

Fortunately for us all, there was a way out of all the problems arising in the Week From Hell. I got a new job within a week or so, testing software for Hewlett Packard again in Fort Collins. The window was pulled and replaced, at my cost. After an expensive overnight stay at the vet, David's dog made a full recovery. We tackled the fails on our inspection one by one and fixed them all.

The main issue was the drywall in the garage. In my inexperience, I had used the 1/2-inch stuff, without knowing that the specs in the garage called for the 5/8-inch fire-rated drywall. After it had been failed, I figured I could just add a 1/4-inch layer to what was already there as this would be cheaper, lighter, and easier to install, especially on the ceiling, but the inspector wouldn't let me go this route.

After a lengthy argument, the county made me add a whole new layer of 1/2-inch drywall to the existing layer of 1/2-inch drywall on the ceiling and walls. It didn't make sense, but after years of struggling with them, I knew I didn't have a choice if I wanted the house to pass.

The county's master electricians actually showed up when

it was time for the second inspection. I had Rachel walk behind them from room to room with her pregnant belly sticking out from under her shirt, wincing and holding her back the whole time for added effect. We passed all the major inspections the second time around.

In the middle of it all, I got the Horse's Ass Award for all the things that I had goofed throughout the course of the year. It was well earned. As the current titleholder, David was in charge of the props and boy, did he deliver. It was a toy model truck with a guy in it that had his fist sticking out the windshield, along with several Popsicle sticks that represented a load of deck timbers that had gone through my actual windshield in a separate mishap.

It was spot on, as I think I went through three windshields in 2009. There was a deer glued to the front of the model, to represent the deer I had clobbered with my car earlier that year. Since I was leaving the house so early every morning, I was constantly having to dodge wildlife on the way into work until finally, I hit something.

Of course, there was also a dog glued to the bottom of the model to represent me running over David's dog, in the Week From Hell. I have to say, I think it was one of the best props ever constructed for the Horse's Ass Award and I still have it to this day. Great job, David!

Anyhow, we made our way through Christmas and New Years, working on the house with every spare second in an effort to get out of the cabin and into our new home. I hired extra help from Craigslist, and together with our friends and my wife's parents, we made the final push. I remember Rachel on her hands and knees grouting the floor of the shower in our bathroom when she was nearly nine months into her pregnancy.

In the end, we got the Certificate of Occupancies to both

structures on February 23rd, 2009. Our son Ben arrived three days later.

* * *

Moving into our new home with our newborn son was one of the most glorious days of my life. I had literally moved fifteen times since leaving my parents' home in 1989 and I was so sick of moving. I had finally fulfilled a life-long dream of building my own house and I was really happy. I can only imagine how good my dad felt, too. With a U.S. government career that spanned thirty-plus years, he frequently had to move to wherever his assignments took him and that meant a lifetime of packing up his and his family's belongings and unpacking them in a rental property, often times in a different country. That must have gotten really old. I'm sure he was more than happy to move his stuff one last time to a new home that was on top of a mountain with gorgeous views in every direction.

The move up the hill was a testament to the hard work and determination we had all put into building these two houses over the previous three years (see photo 2). I took it easy over the next few months as my mind and body slowly healed after three years of upheaval. I focused my attention on advancing Secret Compass, and also my new gig as a vocalist for Peace Officer, a band I had joined in town. It was good to make music again. It seemed like life was going to mellow out for me in the year ahead, but little did I realize the storm that was brewing. I had no idea how hard I'd have to fight to keep our new homes.

* * *

The financial crash of 2008 had come and gone with millions losing their homes, their businesses, and their savings. It was a terrible injustice, but because I had always paid my bills on time and always had verifiable employment, I didn't think it could or would affect me. Little did I know.

I began to catch wind of how the financial landscape had drastically changed in the spring of 2009, when I went to apply for the permanent financing on our two new homes. We had borrowed a substantial amount of money to finance the land, materials, and labor needed to build both of the structures. This was secured with what's known as a construction loan, which was set to expire in June of that year. Usually, the bank that holds the note on construction loans will roll the same note into long-term financing, but for some reason, our bank didn't deal in residential housing.

The construction loan had to be bought out by another financial institution and to my total disbelief, I couldn't find a single bank that would help us. The main problem was that we had built something unique, and there wasn't anything comparable to it within twenty-five miles. It was that simple.

In real estate, value on property is determined by "comparables," meaning that an appraisal is defined according to similar properties within a twenty-five mile radius. This way, if everyone in ownership of the property in question suddenly dies in a plane crash, the bank that owns the property is assured to get what the property is worth when they put the property up for sale.

In a city, this is no problem as there are lots of comparable homes within twenty five miles, but not out in the country and definitely not with a piece of property that had a main home and a "detached garage with accessory living quarters" on it. We had gotten approval from Larimer County through a special hearing to build two homes on one lot, it was perfectly legal, but because no one had built anything similar within a twenty-five mile radius, there were no comparables and no banks would even look at the loan.

I've said it before, and I'll say it again: society just isn't structured for the young to take care of the old anymore. I had built something that would enable us to look after my dad in his golden years, but because no one else had done the same, we couldn't get a loan.

Despite excellent credit scores, despite verifiable income including my dad's federal pension, and despite the fact that I had paid back every nickel I had ever borrowed from anyone dating back to when I was a teenager, every financial institution we approached turned us away.

The deadline on the construction loan came and went. The bank sent us final notices on payment of the full amount due, which of course we didn't have. I scheduled a meeting with the bank, which ended up accomplishing nothing. I pled our case, but it fell on deaf ears. We stared across the table at each other like a couple of alley cats that were about to flip out on one another.

Two weeks later, in between demands for full payment, they filed a late payment notice with the three credit bureaus, so all our credit scores plunged. It was the stupidest thing in the world. They wanted their money, but they were hurting any chance we had to be able to get a loan to get them their money. If we couldn't get a loan with excellent credit scores, how in the hell would we do any better with damaged credit scores?

I steadfastly told the bank that I wasn't going to make any more monthly payments until they removed the late payment notice from our credit reports. They countered by threatening to send the property into foreclosure. I couldn't tell if they were bluffing or not, and that had me on the edge of my seat.

Looking back on it all, I think they were. They knew our

income was stable and that we wanted to keep what we had built, so we had motivation to keep paying the mortgage payments. If they evicted us and put the homes up on the market, how long would they be willing to wait without a payment? And even if they found a buyer, would that prospective buyer even be able to secure a loan? It didn't make sense. I think they saw it the same way.

After two more weeks of the standoff, the bank finally agreed to extend our existing construction loan for a single year. It was a breath of fresh air for all of us. I thought I'd have a solution within a year, for sure; it couldn't be that a stable family with our income wouldn't be able to come up with something. Again, little did I know.

Over the course of the next nine months, we would go through two more appraisals of the property to the tune of around $400 each, and each one of them expired without securing us a loan. We wasted $1,200 and not one financial institution could get past the fact that there was nothing comparable to what we had built within twenty-five miles, despite the fact that the appraisers were independent appraisers that the financial institutions had hired themselves.

We looked into private financing and a variety of other creative options, including moving the Secret Compass office into our house so we could apply for a commercial loan instead of a residential one, but that didn't fly either. I scheduled meetings with mortgage specialists that had never turned me away in the past, in hopes of making the right connection. After getting the initial parameters, they stopped returning phone calls.

I sent the same copies of the same proof of income, credit scores, and the latest appraisals to one bank after another, to no avail. I contacted banks I had done business with before, banks that I had borrowed from and paid back in previous years, and even the local banks, in hopes that one of them would accept the appraisal of our property and one year later, I still had absolutely nothing to show for it.

As we neared the end of the one-year extension, we still didn't have permanent financing. In the last month, I was having difficulty sleeping. I would wake up in cold sweats, panicking over the situation. It was beyond frustrating, especially considering that I was trapped in a job that I was no longer happy with, all because I had to show stable income to any prospective lenders.

There was talk of the bank foreclosing on the property since we still didn't have the money to pay off the construction loan. I am not a violent person by nature, but I can honestly tell you, as I told my wife and my father, there was no way on god's green earth that I was going to pack up and drive away from the two houses we had built, all because we couldn't get these banks to work with us. No way. I broke my back building these two houses and with the incalculable amount of stress I had put myself through, there was no way I was going to go quietly.

I was ready to make the headlines as the first person to resist the millions of foreclosures that had swept across the nation. Then again, I was also so weary from the extended battle that in some ways I was ready to throw in the towel. I know it sounds crazy because I think I *was* crazy at that point. The whole thing had turned me schizoid.

I wanted to fight to keep the houses at all cost, but I also wanted to set them on fire. At one point, I actually called the bank's bluff and told them that we were going to walk away from it all if they pushed us into foreclosure. I was so sick and tired of the game that I was ready to start saying and doing crazy things.

My wife's family has been in Fort Collins for more than

twenty years and considering that Rachel's father is an attorney in town, I didn't think the bank had the guts to foreclose on us when we had the credentials and the means to pay a mortgage. They wouldn't be able to stomach what would certainly be a very newsworthy foreclosure, with a crazy guy like me running his mouth. I could sense it in our conversations leading up to the deadline—they were pressing for a solution that wouldn't get them into hot water.

In the end, believe it or not, they bought out their own loan. In the two to three weeks that followed, they hastily put together a new "jumbo loan" program, and we were the first prospective lenders to qualify for the new program. In June of 2010, after suffering through more than two years' worth of stress and anxiety, we quietly signed the paperwork that converted our expired construction loan into a permanent residential loan, with the *same* bank.

THREE

The Sky's on Fire

With all the global attention Colorado got in the summer of 2012, the destructive fire season that ravaged our mountain community actually did not begin in 2012 at all. In April of 2011, more than a year before what will be remembered as the worst fire season in Colorado history, we had another wildfire come dangerously close to Ohana. It came to be known as the Crystal Mountain Fire, and for many of our neighbors, it was just as destructive.

The blaze began on a mountain more than five miles away from us, started by a caretaker on a ranch who thought it would be a good idea to pour gasoline on a slash pile and ignite it in the middle of a drought and high winds.

The flames quickly spiraled out of control and the genius responsible for it not only fled the scene, but also locked all the gates behind him as he fled. The firefighters that initially responded to the call lost precious time dealing with the gates, and when they arrived, the blaze was out of control.

When it made the news, the Crystal Mountain Fire wasn't considered to be a threat to structures and firefighters were within a day or two of containing the blaze. All that changed one night, thirty hours into it, when the winds suddenly came back full force.

* * *

After the four-year upheaval our family had gone through, building and financing our homes, we had finally settled into what could be considered a normal life and the pursuit of happiness. Once we signed the permanent financing paperwork in June of 2010, I wasted no time in quitting my job and turning my full attention to Secret Compass.

It was a risk, of course, but I could no longer justify giving the best part of my day away to a job that wasn't paying fair market value, wasn't giving raises, and wasn't rewarding hard work. I walked away and never looked back.

Within three months of going to work full time for myself, I got my company to a point where I simply couldn't get up earlier or get it all done by dinnertime, so I hired my first two employees. They were good friends of mine and I came up with a plan that guaranteed their paychecks and offered them both a really good sales commission.

Together, the three of us quickly outgrew the garage on Mason Street, where I had spent the last five years urinating into Gatorade bottles. I'm not kidding. The garage had no heat, no air conditioning, and no bathroom. I managed to keep it going all those years with a space heater and a window mounted AC unit, but both were really ineffective. I froze all winter and sweated all summer.

Three was a crowd in the garage—there wasn't even any room for us to work, and it was clear that no one was going to share my Gatorade bottles. Within a couple of months we moved our company to a proper office and warehouse complex. It actually had a bathroom, which in itself was a luxury.

Behind the scenes, life couldn't have been better. Rachel and I were having the time of our lives watching Baby Ben get bigger with each passing day. In our close-knit family community, Rachel's mom was there to help whenever we needed anything and both our fathers were right there beside us as well.

I think Ben has to be the only child in the whole state of Colorado with his grandmother and both grandfathers all living together on the same piece of property. That's 195 years' worth of experience, right there for Ben when he needs it. We felt empowered and blessed that our decision to create a family homestead years prior had blossomed into such a success. Ohana was giving back after all the years that we had given to it.

Personally, I was doing great. The company was taking off, and I was really happy to see something I had worked so hard on for so long finally be able to support my family.

In accordance with my innate inability to never stay idle, I had two projects going at once up at Ohana. I had begun renovating the cabin Rachel and I had lived in for three years, and I was also working on finishing the basement in our new house. Neither project had a deadline and that made all the difference in the world in terms of stress levels. I hired my friends to get the jobs done and we worked at a comfortable pace. Both projects were easy going and rewarding.

I was writing lyrics and playing shows regularly as a vocalist with Peace Officer. In addition, I managed to finish a science fiction novel I'd been working on over the past three to four years and had self-published it through a hybrid publishing and marketing firm. Between music and writing, I had two creative outlets and that made me feel balanced. I also had time to hang out with my friends and family again, which I had really missed. Everything was going great.

I was working on the lyrics to a new Peace Officer track late one night when we got word of the firestorm headed our way. It was just after midnight and my family was asleep. The track I was working on was a bit haunting and I'd literally just written down the first sentence, "The sky's on fire and I feel like I'm dying..." when suddenly the phone rang. It was my neighbor. She simply said, "Look up at the mountain behind you."

I ran to the window and I couldn't believe my eyes. The entire top of the mountain just behind Ohana was engulfed in flames. I watched in horror as two trucks pulling horse trailers abruptly shot out of the smoke.

They were barreling down a dirt access road that was the only means of escape from a cluster of houses on the other side of the ridge. The horses were being thrown against the insides of the trailers like pinballs as the drivers careened around the curves of the road. They were running for their lives.

I didn't even have a chance to collect my thoughts before the phone rang again. It was the reverse 911 call, which is an automated phone call you get from emergency dispatchers regarding a potential disaster area with instructions on evacuation. It was a mandatory evacuation.

I immediately ran to the master bedroom and woke up Rachel. We made a quick plan and then both went to work. I organized all the photo albums, cameras, laptops, and computer towers into a pile by the door while she got Ben up and started packing clothes.

Just as I stepped outside to load up the vehicles, an explosion suddenly ripped through the night sky just south of us. Somebody's propane tank had detonated; the liquid fuel shot it fifty to a hundred feet into the air like a missile. I stared in disbelief as gravity slowed the tank's thrust to a crawl, and then slowly pulled the ball of flames back to Earth.

The wind was gusting at 40 to 50 miles an hour, pushing heavily from the northwest to the southeast behind my dad's house. I could see the flames spreading in the trees south of him. It was a firestorm and it was out of control. Rachel appeared moments later with a couple of suitcases, a groggy Ben, and an update. Everyone on the ranch had received the reverse 911 call and there would be a rendezvous at the mailboxes in fifteen minutes.

I ferried the photo albums and computers into the trunk of Rachel's SUV before running back into the house to call my dad. To my utter disbelief, he refused to evacuate with the rest of us. I pleaded with him to leave, but no matter what I said, he still wouldn't budge.

I was out of time so I began screaming threats and obscenities into the phone in an effort to persuade him. The old man from Brooklyn had heard it all before and he wasn't moved by my poetry. I slammed the phone down in disgust and switched gears back to the evacuation.

I corralled our cat, his food, and his litter box into my car before doing a final run through our house. It's hard to put into words how nauseating this "final run" feels. For anyone that has ever been evacuated due to weather conditions or an emergency that is hell bent on obliterating your home and everything in it, you know what I mean. It's a cocktail of anxiety, depression, and fear boiling in your stomach as you race from room to room.

The clock is ticking in the back of your mind like you're

in some kind of demented game show. You're rapidly scanning through your belongings, trying to decide what's important enough for you to grab, but the truth of it is that you want to grab *all* your belongings; it's just that you can't because you're out of time. You have to leave immediately and you have to make some hard choices.

In the end, I grabbed a few of my old T-shirts and two picture frames with snapshots of my mom and dad before vacating the house for the last time. By the time we got to the rendezvous point at the bottom of our driveway, everything to the immediate south and southeast of Ohana was on fire. It was spreading quickly.

I knew that my dad would have the sense to leave if the flames got too close, but nevertheless, I was worried sick. Smoke inhalation can be fatal and it could overwhelm him before he even had a chance to react. I was scared to death that something would go wrong and I would never see my dad again, and I was angry at myself that I had not done enough to make him evacuate along with us. I absolutely did not want to leave without him, but I had to make sure that Rachel and Ben got to safety. Words cannot describe the conflict churning in my head.

The turmoil was punctuated by a flood of emergency vehicles that suddenly went screaming by us. One of the fire trucks abruptly pulled off the county road and jerked to a stop beside the mailboxes. I got out and ran up to the driver, who looked like he was in his mid-twenties. I could see the raw fear in his eyes.

I proceeded to tell him that my dad had refused to leave, and gave him rough directions to my dad's house at the top of the driveway. I didn't know if that meant the firefighters would pay special attention to our property or not, but I had to at least tell them that we had left a man behind.

We were directed to leave immediately via the northerly

route, which took us to a vantage point above Ohana as the road wound up into the mountains toward Rist Canyon. The scene behind us was absolutely terrifying. Everything just south of our beautiful valley was on fire.

The high winds were pushing the blaze farther south, but if they changed direction, Ohana was only five hundred feet from the flames. It was so precariously close, with the fate of it all literally hanging in the wind. All we had built, and all our hard work over the past six years...it was all on the line.

I was consumed with anxiety and despair. I desperately wanted to turn around and go back to defend my home and to make sure my dad would make it to safety if the flames came for what was his, but I had to think of Ben and Rachel first. It took everything in me to keep driving. I prayed that everything would be okay as the firestorm faded to black in my rearview mirror.

* * *

We stayed on some couches in the Secret Compass warehouse that night. I tried to get some sleep like the rest of my family, but I just couldn't. I was too worried. The ramifications of losing everything were too much to bear. I finally feel asleep sometime around 3:00 a.m. after tossing and turning for much of the night.

I called my dad as soon as I opened my eyes the next morning. We had gotten extremely lucky. Not only had the fire pushed past us, but overnight, a weather system had miraculously moved into the area. Apparently, it was snowing. I ran out into the street in my underwear and literally jumped for joy in my bare feet. I've never been so happy to see snow fall like that in all of my life.

The firefighters had worked through the night to contain the blaze and the storm front had really helped. By the next morning, they were at more than 60 percent containment, but there were still parts of the fire that were out of control—3,000 acres and counting. The police had checkpoints set up on the roads going to and from the burn area; they weren't letting anyone in, not even residents. I managed to talk my way through by explaining to the cops that my dad had not evacuated and I had to check on him.

Everyone was on pins and needles for the next few days as the fire crews worked overtime to fully contain the blaze. The choppers clattered up and down the canyon for hours on end, investigating hot spots and then dumping water on them. We were evacuated one other time later that week when the fire flared up again, but by the following day, the firefighters announced that they were at 100 percent containment.

Somehow, some way, Ohana had escaped unscathed. The firestorm had blown right past us along the southern property line and had caused no damage. Thirteen of our neighbors were not so lucky. All of the homes on the ridge behind our house were gone. Linda Masterson, best known for her book *Living With Bears: A Practical Guide to Bear Country*, and her husband, Cory, lost their home and grounds along with four or five other families. Linda has since written a new book based on her experience called *Surviving Wildfire: Get Prepared, Stay Alive, Rebuild Your Life (A Handbook for Homeowners)*.

My friends Curt and Kelly saw the fire coming from more than two miles away and still had less than ten minutes to gather what few precious belongings they could get into their cars before the wind-driven flames overwhelmed them. They lost everything, and I do mean everything.

They lost their home and everything in it, along with a guest home with everything in it, a truck with a plow on it, a backhoe, and a late model PT Cruiser, among other things. Curt converts old diesels to run on vegetable oil in his spare time so he had a few project cars parked on his property, including three Mercedes diesels. The Crystal Mountain Fire took them all.

We hosted a benefit at Ohana two weeks later and helped raise over $10,000 in donations that went to the victims. I'll never forget the moment that Curt and Kelly arrived. I ran to their truck and wrapped my arms around them both like they were the last two human beings on Earth. I wanted to cry too, but I knew if I started, I wouldn't stop. It had been such a harrowing experience for everyone. I can't even imagine coming home to what they came home to.

We insisted that Curt and Kelly stay with us for the next couple of months while they got back on their feet, and they accepted. They moved into one of the guest cabins at Ohana. A few days later, I accompanied them back to their property to help them start the clean-up and I couldn't believe what I saw. It was absolutely nuclear, like the surface of a black moon.

All that remained of the houses were crumbling foundations and everything in them was reduced to ash. All their clothes, furniture, electronic equipment, and personal effects were simply gone. The larger appliances were barely recognizable as appliances. The big trees on the grounds were so scorched that they looked like black-lighted caricatures of themselves, their branches solemnly trapped in time like iron spires on a cathedral.

There were more than six vehicles on the property and they were all incinerated. The fire had burned so hot that the wheels on the PT Cruiser were reduced to tiny aluminum rivers.

Like many people who build homes in the mountains, Curt built with the potential destruction by wildfires in mind. The structures he built both had stone exteriors and metal roofs, which supposedly will help repel fire because these materials aren't flammable. As we would all come to learn, none of that really matters when you're dealing with a fire driven by high winds. I heard the term "fireball" used more than once by my neighbors.

At one of the burn sites, I noticed that the lawn and the wooden fence leading right up to the residence were virtually unscathed, but the house burned down anyway. I'm talking about a house standing in the middle of a prairie, with no trees and hundreds of feet of defensible space surrounding it.

The problem is, with a firestorm like this, it doesn't matter if you build with materials that aren't flammable or you cut down the trees close to your house. None of that matters anymore. The fireball blasts out your windows and sets the stuff *inside* your house on fire, so it burns down from the inside out. All you can do in a situation like this is get your loved ones to safety and then pray.

When the dust settled, thirteen of our neighbors had lost their homes. After staying with us for a month or so, Curt and Kelly moved into a smaller place farther down Buckhorn Canyon, with hopes to one day rebuild what the Crystal Mountain Fire took from them. I don't think anyone on the ridge behind Ohana is going to rebuild; most of the people that lost structures vacated their land and moved away.

It was sad to see our community lose friends and neighbors in such a shocking turn of events. There was a real sense of concern at Ohana over the forecasted droughts in the years to come and the wildfires that might accompany them.

We were lucky enough to have the RCVFD (Rist Canyon Volunteer Fire Department) over in the next canyon, but with a firestorm, there's little that any fire department can do. Besides, even if they could help, their trucks were still twenty minutes away.

We talked a lot about the preventive measures we could take at Ohana to better protect ourselves in the future. Keeping trees and grass trimmed back from structures was a given, as was being extra careful with anything flammable. We mulled over a handful of new ideas, including installing storm shutters on all our windows and installing a system of pumps and hoses that could pull water from the lake to protect our homes in case another wildfire passed through.

The truth of it is, we really didn't put any of these ideas into action. We got preoccupied with the summer ahead, we got comfortable, and we got complacent. It's so easy to push your fears out of your mind when the sun rises and falls on life here in our beloved valley. Behind it all, though, our fears were justified.

Ohana was vulnerable, particularly from the northwest. The storms and prevailing winds almost always pushed in from the mountains to the northwest of us and if a fire ever got started in those mountains, the winds would push it right onto our property. We were sitting ducks.

I suppose it sat in the backs of all our minds as we went about our daily lives, but no one ever really thought our community could or would see the same type of disaster unfold again, any time soon. Certainly not any time soon, right? Certainly not a disaster ten to twenty times as bad, just a year later, right?

FOUR

Embers

The High Park Fire was first reported at daybreak on Saturday morning, June 9th, 2012. It started as a plume of smoke not more than two miles to the northwest of our property. To understand the events that would unfold throughout the course of this day, I have to take you back in time a week or so to fully comprehend the scene at Ohana.

* * *

Our mountain community was already on high alert. The winter snows were meager for 2011, and the rain we expected in the spring of 2012 was nothing to get excited about either. That left us with a very dry start to the summer season, less than a year after the Crystal Mountain Fire had ravaged our community, and a very dry forest.

The pine beetles had already killed many trees and were threatening many more. There were dead trees by the thousands in the forests west of Fort Collins and that meant an almost inexhaustible source of fuel should there ever be a spark.

It didn't take long for the sirens to start wailing. On May 14th, a camper hiking on one of the trails in nearby Poudre Canyon knocked over his cook stove and ignited what would come to be known as the Hewlett Gulch Wildfire. This was about ten miles away from Ohana, but considering everything we had recently learned about how quickly wind-driven fires can move, we were especially nervous.

In the end, the blaze scorched 7,600 acres of forested land and took eight days to contain. Fortunately, despite hundreds of evacuations, no homes were lost, but it left everyone in the mountain communities on edge.

* * *

Rachel and I were still concentrating our efforts on two projects at home. We were simultaneously trying to finish the basement in our new house and also trying to renovate the cabin that we had lived in for three years.

The latter ended up being a real source of stress. The problem was, earlier in the year, we had committed the cabin to a private yoga retreat for family and friends that would begin on June 7th, but by the end of May, we weren't even close to being finished.

There would be seventeen guests camping on the property for the next three weeks and our cabin was to be their meeting hall and also their main bathroom. We had less than a week to go before the retreat was set to start and the cabin wasn't ready.

I found myself under the gun, yet again, working day and night to try and finish a project with a major deadline looming over us. It was a predicament that I had grown to despise over the past ten years of building and renovating houses—the deadline at the end and the overwhelming stress and lack of sleep that came with it.

In that last week with the cabin, I would work all day for Secret Compass, then shop for materials for the next two hours, then drive a truckload of materials back to Ohana, then work until one in the morning on the various unfinished projects, then repeat the same thing all over again, five hours later.

I was so tired of going to Home Depot and tired of the cycle of estimating what I needed, then returning all the things that ended up not working, with a fistful of receipts to keep track of, that I always lost track of. After years and years and years of building and renovations, I just didn't have it in me anymore. It was a relentless schedule that quickly wore me out, but it didn't leave me with much of a choice. If I wanted to have the cabin ready for the retreat when it started, I had to stick with it.

Some of our guests actually showed up a couple of days early, which put added pressure on us because there was still so much left to do and we only had two days to finish. Then on the 6th of June, the last night before the retreat was set to start, we got hit with a sudden thunderstorm that had moved into the mountains. The storm was met with open arms.

Aside from the much-needed precipitation, the downpour seemed to cleanse the air of the stress that hung over Ohana. We were ready to put the grueling schedule of the last month behind us, and our guests were ready to get the three-week yoga session underway with a fresh start.

The rain came down in buckets as we worked late into the night on our last minute preparations of the cabin. Little did we know, as the lightning struck and struck often, of the demon that nature was giving birth to less than two miles away from our property.

We had a tough time explaining the Larimer County-mandated fire ban to our guests when the yoga retreat began the next day. Naturally, when people are camping, they want to build a campfire. It goes hand and hand with mountain retreats in general, for comfort and also for ambience. We sat our guests down for an orientation that we put together to get them acquainted with the grounds and the common precautions that come with living in the mountains, but the fact that it had rained the night before had some of them questioning the fire ban.

We did our best to try and explain the situation to them. The Hewlett Gulch Wildfire had barely been contained not two weeks prior and the community was really on edge. The candles our guests were lighting as part of the yoga sessions were already a hazard, and we could not risk anything else with an open flame.

As the retreat got underway, we continued to prepare the grounds for what would be a three-week stay for seventeen guests. That night, Rachel headed down to the Summer Art Market in Denver for the weekend and I came down with the flu. It was no surprise, I suppose, with the schedule I had kept over the last two weeks.

I had worked myself to the bone while averaging four to five hours of sleep a night for days on end and had not eaten well because I was so busy. We managed to finish the cabin on time, but I was utterly exhausted, both mentally and physically.

Unfortunately, I barely got any sleep that night either, as I tossed and turned with a severe head cold that kept me up. I got out of bed the next morning feeling just as exhausted as the moment I had laid down and closed my eyes. It was a Saturday and I knew that we would be celebrating Lisa's birthday at Ohana later in the day with a bunch of family members that were on the way.

I was so tired and weak from the flu that all I wanted to do, more than anything, was to go back to sleep. It was an exhaustion that felt like it needed twelve hours of sleep a night for the next two weeks, but that wasn't going to happen. Little did I know, my sleepless nights had just begun.

The phone rang just after breakfast and my attention was drawn to a plume of smoke on the horizon to the northwest of us. I stood there on the deck and stared at it in disbelief. As the entire world would come to realize in the days ahead, the thunderstorm we had applauded two nights prior had ushered in a demon.

The lightning that came with the storm found its way to the earth's surface, to a single tree on the mountain just north of a small community known as High Park.

Despite the rains that came with the storm, the burning embers persevered. Despite the volume of water that came down on this single tree, the burning embers persevered. In the two days that followed, if another storm had come through, or a late season frost had come through, the embers might have been extinguished, but the universe didn't provide either of those things, so the embers persevered.

For the next two days those tiny sparks plotted and conspired until finally, on the morning of June 9th, they came out of the shadows of doubt with a roar. The micron and the nanosecond; how delicately they mold fate.

I just stood there on the deck outside my house, staring in silence at the plume of smoke to the northwest. I couldn't believe it. It was the one place that I had prayed I would never see smoke. Ohana was now shockingly vulnerable to the wind that typically pushed in from the higher mountains. All that we had worked for was now threatened.

I stood there thinking about the struggle we had gone through over the last seven years; all the days and nights I had worked until I was too tired to even keep my eyes open, the stress, the anxiety, and the lack of sleep that came with trying to build two homes at once, forty-five minutes from town, in the mountains.

The river of time flooded my mind as I stood there and watched the plume of smoke gain strength (see photo 3). I tried to imagine a scenario where the fire crews would have the blaze contained by lunchtime, and life would just go on as if nothing had ever happened. The planes that began circling the growing inferno in the distance snapped me out of my daydream.

The smoke quietly overtook the light to the northwest, and before long, it had completely consumed the skyline. I went down to the yoga circle and brought our guests up to date. I tried to sound hopeful, as if the emergency vehicles screaming by our property on the county road were going to take care of everything.

Within the hour, our family began to arrive to celebrate Lisa's birthday. Everyone was concerned with the gloom on the horizon and unfortunately, it dominated the afternoon. We tried to go about the plan for the day despite what was happening. We ate cake and Lisa opened her presents as updates came in via the web.

It was not looking good. The fire had expanded greatly to the north for the time being, that much was clear. The problem was, because it was all so new, there weren't any hard stats on the homes that were in danger or the acreage that had been lost.

The view from my dad's place at the top of Ohana confirmed that the blaze had grown immensely throughout the course of the day, but without an official assessment, we were basically in the dark. I had no idea if the fire was something that could or would be easily contained or if it was totally out of control.

My head was pounding with the flu and all I wanted to do was go back to sleep. Once I got back to my house, I set my son up with a video and attempted to take a nap. I fell asleep for maybe half an hour when the phone rang. The voice on the other end of the phone was a voice I didn't want to hear.

It was the reverse 911 call that I had hoped and prayed we would not be getting. It was a mandatory evacuation. I held the phone to my ear long after the automated message had ended, long after the dial tone came back on and then eventually switched off again, into the oblivion of my mind.

The woman's voice on the emergency recording had sounded a lot like that woman's voice at the end of the movie *Aliens*, giving the countdown for what would be the nuclear explosion that eradicated the LV-426 colony: "…all personnel must evacuate immediately. You now have just four minutes to reach minimum safe distance…"

I felt like I was in a trance. I wondered if the parallel in my mind was a coincidence, or a sign of what was to come. Would Ohana go the way of LV-426? The two female voices seemed to be the same, and I was straining to remember if the first woman's voice in my head was even real, or if it was a figment of my imagination.

My whole body ached. I was at the tipping point between reality and fiction, the edge of dreamland, amplified by the delirium that I experience when I have the flu or serious stress. It's been that way for me ever since I was a kid. Fragments of memories come and go from different times in my life as I drift in and out of consciousness. I wrote the phone call off as a lucid dream that was driven by my fears of what was happening to the northwest of our homes.

I had just gotten comfortable with the idea that Ms. Countdown from *Aliens* was trying to exploit my fears and trick me in my dreams when the phone rang again. It was Lisa. She wanted to let me know that everyone on the ranch was preparing to evacuate and how much time would I need to meet up with them?

I mumbled something into the phone and then threw it against the wall. A third woman's voice and it was decidedly not Ms. Countdown. It was my mother-in-law and it was real.

I gritted my teeth and opened my eyes. There was no denying it. The first phone call and the second phone call were both unequivocally real. I couldn't just roll over and go back to sleep, as badly as I wanted to. The reality of the situation slowly began to filter into my mind.

In the next few minutes, we would not only have to evacuate everyone who lived at Ohana along with our extended family that had come for Lisa's birthday party, but also the seventeen guests that were camping on the property as part of the yoga retreat.

It was too much to bear. I had a thousand spears suddenly jut into my brain, all at once. I was overwhelmed with the flood of decisions I would have to make in the minutes ahead, apprehensive of the confrontational phone call I would soon be having with my dad, embarrassed to face our seventeen guests because the yoga retreat would now be deemed a total failure, disgusted with the fire, fearful of the inevitable southeast winds, and angry with the universe.

Really, universe????? I get sick once or twice a year, and you know when I do that it's bad, so after weeks on end of working my ass off, sleeping little, eating bad, and feeling totally exhausted, this is what you give me when I come down with the flu.???? This is what I get???? I was enraged. My head was a hand grenade, ready to blow.

Obviously, the planets had aligned many times in my life to give me victories when I was struggling and needed help. I had praised the universe then, when it spun my way, but in the heat of this moment, I could not see the balance in it all. I was out of my mind.

With utter contempt for everything, I finally threw back the covers and flung myself out of bed. I marched down the hallway and peered at the horizon to the northwest. The county road that meandered past Ohana up into the hills was teeming with emergency vehicles.

I picked up the phone and called my dad, who again refused to evacuate with the rest of us. Somehow, I knew that was coming and I didn't even have the strength to fight with him. In a robotic state, I began to assemble the same pile of photo albums and computers by the front door, exactly as I had done the year before. The inside of my head was so scorched with contempt that I had gone to autopilot. I felt like a cyborg.

I went into the bathroom and splashed water on my face. I stared at myself in the mirror…*Snap out of it, Cooper.* I desperately tried to push it all out of my mind for the sake of my son and the rest of my family. I took a few deep breaths and then began loading up the car.

Lisa and a few other members of our family came up to check on me to see if I needed help, but I shrugged them off. I can't really explain why I was so adamant to do it all myself. I can be hard to deal with when I'm really frustrated. I got Ben squared away in his car seat and then loaded up Stanley, our cat, along with his food and litter box.

I ran back into the house and made my way down the stairs

to the basement. I had just poured two years of my life into completing the entertainment center there and I hadn't even gotten a chance to insure it all.

There were countless irreplaceable things from different phases of my life...photos, posters, statues, DVDs, camera/video/audio equipment, tour diaries from my time on the road with my bands, notebooks filled with lyrics and songs...I was so overwhelmed with the thought of losing it all, but there simply wasn't enough time to grab everything, or enough space to stow it even if I had the time. I felt like putting my head through one of the walls.

In the last few seconds, I hurriedly snapped a few photos with my phone, grabbed a poster frame loaded up with all my old concert ticket stubs, and headed back up the stairs. I made sure all the windows and doors were shut before closing the front door behind me. I paused and stared at my house before getting into my car. *You nearly killed me, you sonofabitch, you'd better be here when I come back.* The fear was boiling in my mind like a cauldron over a roaring fire.

I drove down my driveway and made my way to an area on the property where most of our guests taking part in the retreat were camping. They had already evacuated, all of them, in three cars. David and Lisa were waiting for me by the cabin.

I realized in a flash that the cabin's insurance policy had not been updated to include all the materials and hard work Rachel and I had put into renovating it over the past year. My friend Jeff had spent the last six months painstakingly adding ornate trim to various parts of the interior, among a thousand other things, and there I stood without a proper insurance policy to cover the loss if everything went up in smoke. What a goddamned genius I was.

I barely heard David and Lisa as they reviewed the final

evacuation plan and the rendezvous point in town. I abruptly realized that there was a propane tank hanging on a barbeque grill next to the cabin. This would be a ticking time bomb, not four feet from the structure, if the fire made it onto our property. I hurriedly unscrewed the tank and relocated it. Unfortunately, in the thirty seconds it took me to do this, my son managed to roll down his car window just enough for Stanley to escape. I desperately lunged after the cat, but he made it into the thick brush next to the cabin and there was no hope of getting him out.

We had to leave immediately and simply couldn't wait the hours it would take for the cat to resurface at home. Ben was crying and screaming from the backseat of the car for me to get Stanley, but we were out of time. The tension was too much to bear. I *literally* began ramming my fists into the sides of my head, as hard as I could.

The last few minutes at Ohana are kind of a blur to me now. I think the reshuffled plan was that David and Lisa would wait another half an hour or so to see if Stanley would make his way back to our house and I would get Ben to safety. I knew that this would be futile as the cat wouldn't head home until nightfall, but I didn't want to argue. I got back in my car and cleared out.

I remember driving past a handful of emergency vehicles as I made my way down the canyon, but that's all I remember. At some point I spoke to David via my cell phone and he told me they were evacuating without Stanley. We were all supposed to meet up in town later, but in the heat of the moment, all of that changed. It doesn't make sense as I sit here now, looking back on that day; I'm not sure anything I did during this evacuation made any sense.

I got it in my head that I had to go back to Ohana and save

Stanley. I knew that the cat would return by nightfall and if no one was home to let him in, we ran the risk that he would not be alive in the morning. In Colorado, there are mountain lions, bobcats, foxes, and coyotes waiting for the opportunity to gobble up your wayward pet and I couldn't have our cat becoming a statistic. I wouldn't be able to face myself, let alone my wife and son, if I didn't do something. By the time I drove into Fort Collins, I had a new mission and I wasted no time in implementing it.

Instead of going to the Secret Compass warehouse as planned, I took Ben to stay the night with some friends that had offered to share their home with us. After kissing him goodnight, I climbed back into my car and stomped on the gas pedal. I was doing around ninety when I flashed by David and Lisa as they were coming down the canyon; our cars passed just outside of Masonville. I didn't even slow down. They must have thought I was crazy to be heading back into it.

I got back home right around nightfall and of course, Stanley was waiting right by the front door. I knew he would be. Our cat is smart enough to know where the food is when he's hungry. I quietly let him in and made my way to the deck to see what had happened on the horizon in my absence.

Much to my dismay, I could actually see the flames. The fire had advanced southeast toward Ohana in the last hour. I stood there and stared as the wind pushed hard against my face. The southeast winds were driving the inferno toward our homes, as I had anticipated, should we ever be confronted with a fire to the northwest of us.

My heart was aching in my chest. I'm at a loss to explain the next couple of hours except to say that I was in a very dark place. For all the people that have come and gone from my life, friends and family members that really know me, you have seen me through some crazy moments in the last twenty years and I'm saying it with all sincerity: out of all the darkness you've helped me survive, this was one of the darkest moments in my life. I really believed that we would lose our home and everything in it. The overwhelming feeling of hopelessness I was experiencing can be attributed to reactive depression, a psychiatric condition that runs in my blood. It is triggered by severe life events, and I have had to actively work my whole life to keep from falling into darkness, in moments like this. This is where it lurks, waiting like a spider to spring out of the shadows and strip all the light from a situation that is already bleak to begin with.

For anyone that knows this kind of depression, you know what I mean. Any hope you might normally be able to muster is replaced by a powerful hopelessness. The thing is, I'm not one for hopelessness, even if I've conjured it up myself. It makes me feel cornered and when I feel cornered, I go ballistic. I made a crazy decision right then and there, in the delirium of those deep, dark thoughts. I wasn't going to leave. I was going to go down fighting with the ship.

I know it sounds insane, but in the disillusionment of it all, it somehow felt like it was to be my destiny. I stood on the deck and stared at the flames. The wind forced tears from my eyes and I defiantly wiped them away with my sleeve as quickly as they appeared.

I stomped back into the kitchen and got to work preparing my favorite meal, pasta with seafood. *Frutti di mare*, as we say in Italian. Forty-five minutes later, I had a piping hot pot of linguini, clams, shrimp, and mussels.

Normally, since I watch my weight, I try and limit myself to a single serving size whenever I make this dish. Not on this night. The fire was coming and I didn't give a shit. I figured if I was going to die fighting to save my home, at least I was going to do it with a belly full of my favorite food.

I positioned my chair so I could watch the flames from the table and then sat down with a giant bowl of frutti di mare, a glass of white wine, and a fork. I proceeded to knock off almost the entire pound of pasta, plus the seafood. When I could eat no more, I pushed back the bowl and went back to staring at the fire through the window.

I started to make mental notes on how far the garden hose in the back of the house would reach, and the most effective ways to make use of a single fire extinguisher. Eventually, as my eyelids got heavy, I began to see the futility of it all. I wasn't making sense. Thankfully, within a few minutes, I fell asleep at the table with my head in my hands.

I woke up a couple of hours later. I had dreamt of Rachel and Ben, and the dream had given me a renewed sense of clarity. I began to review my plan and my thoughts. It was all starting to unravel. Did I really want to risk my life for the house? Was I really considering the reality of my wife having to continue as a widow and my son having to grow up without his father if I died fighting an inferno instead of evacuating like everyone else?

I played out the opening stages of both scenarios in my mind and then got really pissed off at myself. Custer's last stand didn't make sense anymore, and I was somewhat ashamed that this had even registered as a viable option to me.

I don't know if it was time, the food, the sleep, or a combination of the three, but the darkness that had ruled over this predicament with an iron fist was no longer in control. It had passed, and light was beginning to creep in around the edges. I was starting to think more clearly.

I went out on the deck and checked the horizon. Somehow,

the flames had not advanced. The burn line was exactly where it was when I fell asleep. The wind was still blowing pretty hard, but I couldn't tell what effect it was having on the fire. It had not advanced toward Ohana in the last two hours, and that gave me hope.

I came to the conclusion that although I was stressed out of my head, decisively, there was not much that I could personally do about it. I suppose that's exactly the same conclusion that almost everyone else had come to hours earlier when they quietly packed what few things they could and evacuated. Once, not twice. I thought about checking in with my dad before I left, but I figured it would only lead to a fight. I was 100% certain he would not evacuate, no matter what I said, and I was too tired to argue. I piled the dishes in the sink, loaded up the cat, and drove back to Fort Collins.

In my mind, I justified the return trip as the trip to save the cat. It would comfort everyone, especially my son. Had I not returned, I honestly don't know what would have happened to Stanley. Despite the demented episode, the trip did have some merit. I was still anxious and scared, but I knew that my wife and son would still need me in the morning, whether Ohana burned to the ground or not.

* * *

The next two days were pandemonium for the city of Fort Collins. The crisis quickly became headline news in the Northern Colorado community, then the entire country, and then the world. The inferno raging in the mountains just to the northwest of Ohana had exploded into an all out siege on man and nature. It had incinerated more than a hundred structures in forty-eight hours as people living in the mountain communities west of Fort Collins fled for their lives.

One woman didn't make it out fast enough; the cabin she was living in was annihilated before she could escape and she perished in the flames. Entire square miles were scorched in a matter of hours.

I couldn't believe my eyes when I saw a picture in the newspaper, not two days later, of a house on the edge of Fort Collins that fire crews were struggling to save. I stared at the photo in disbelief. That home was twenty miles away from where the fire started. It had advanced twenty miles, all the way to the edge of the city, in less than forty-eight hours. That was beyond imagination.

The firestorm had come up and over Rist Canyon, and had blown right through it like a cyclone. All of that with zero containment. I wondered if houses in Fort Collins would catch fire. We were in desperate need of manpower and equipment to combat the inferno. The local fire crews were overwhelmed, and it would take another three or fours days for the country to mobilize. In that time period, the High Park Fire quickly became the most destructive wildfire in the history of Larimer County.

Rachel was in the middle of the Summer Art Market down in Denver, one of the most important art shows of the year, when she got word of the crisis. There wasn't much she could do from afar as we evacuated Ohana.

She was so worried, though, that she was ready to pack up all her paintings and head back to Fort Collins just to be with Ben and me, but I convinced her to keep her booth open and finish the show. After all the work she had put into preparing for the market, it wouldn't do her or anyone else any good to have her miss out on a chance to sell her paintings.

All the same, I can't imagine it was easy, trying to cheerfully discuss art while sitting there on pins and needles the whole time. Ben and I headed down to Denver on Sunday evening and helped her pack up her car when the market closed down. Despite all the offers we had from friends and family who opened their homes to us, we came back to Fort Collins and set up temporary quarters in the Secret Compass warehouse, until we could come up with a better plan.

We stayed there the next few days as the crisis expanded exponentially. The skies quickly filled with planes and helicopters as fire fighters and heavy equipment began to arrive from across the nation to help local fire crews combat the blaze. Even with reinforcements, five days into the crisis, the news channels were still reporting zero percent containment. The fire was completely out of control, and spreading at an alarming rate.

The smoke was so thick in Fort Collins that we could barely breathe. People wondered if the fire crews could keep the city safe. Everyone was glued to their laptops, refreshing computer-generated topographic "fire maps" that showed the advancing burn lines.

I was on the phone with my dad every two hours in an effort to keep up with what he could see and hear back at Ohana. Since he had refused to evacuate, he was able to at least provide me with the latest information from the front lines. It killed two birds with one stone. I didn't have to worry about his personal well-being since we were in constant communication and his updates really helped quell my fears. I would call or text the rest of our family right after speaking with him.

In the first few days, the High Park Fire had literally advanced in every direction *except* southeast, despite the southeast winds pushing against it. It had scorched thousands of acres in every other direction, but not southeast. The fire actually went against the wind, due to the strong fuel sources to the north, east, and west. It was incomprehensible. It gave my family hope that Ohana would be spared. Again.

The problem was, the fire couldn't and wouldn't ignore the fuel to the southeast forever. It was fantasy to imagine that it would, and I didn't even realize it at the time. Little did I know what was coming in the days ahead.

1) The Ditch, spring of 2007.

2) Both houses, spring of 2009.

3) The morning the High Park Fire started.

4) An Erickson S-64 Air Crane Helitanker,
sucking water out of our lake.

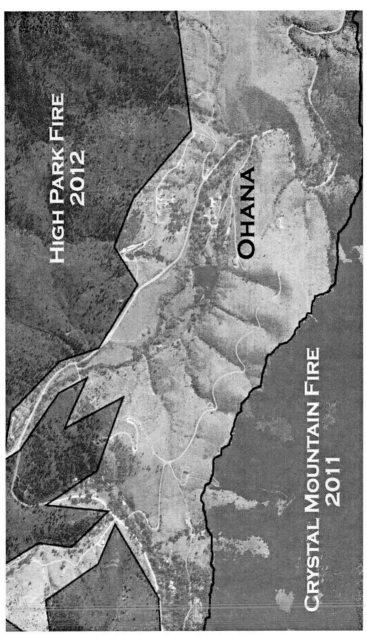

5) The burn lines of both wildfires.

Aftermath of the High Park Fire, one year later.

FIVE

June 12th, 2012

June 12th, 2012, will be a day I remember for the rest of my life. Once you have read this chapter…you'll understand why. It all began around 7:00 a.m., when I tried to reach my dad to get an update on the fire. His phone went straight to voice mail—it didn't even ring once. That could only mean one thing, which I confirmed by calling Poudre Valley REA, the utility service that provides electricity to the mountain communities outside Fort Collins. Due to the advancing wildfire, the fire departments had asked Poudre Valley REA to cut the power to everything up Buckhorn Canyon.

That translated to a whole host of things at Ohana that would consequently stop functioning. First, no phones. Second, no Internet, as all the modems and routers run on electricity. Third, no new water, as the pumps in the wells run on electricity.

We have a cistern on the property that we installed when we built the two new homes on the mountain, which meant that the ranch would still have two thousand gallons to use in the event of a power outage, but my dad's place sits above this cistern. He has a pump that draws the water uphill, but without electricity, this pump will not run and that means no water will flow out of his faucets if there is no electrical service.

With Internet and phone out of commission as well, I had absolutely no way of getting in touch with my dad. In a panic, I got online and checked the fire map. I winced as the map rendered and came into full view on my monitor. The fire had advanced southeast overnight. It was dangerously close to Ohana, which meant that the smoke had to be overwhelming. I started freaking out, wondering if my dad was just going to out-stubborn the fire or if he was in fact passed out on the floor from smoke inhalation.

Either way, I had lost contact with him and that was eating me alive. I started turning it over and over in my mind and I came to the conclusion that I needed to get up to Ohana as soon as possible, but the problem was that the police had set up checkpoints on all the roads leading to and from the burn zone. The whole mountain community west of Fort Collins was on total lock down.

Sometime later that morning, I spoke to David. I told him that I was going to try and talk my way through the checkpoint, in hopes of getting back to Ohana to get my dad. He advised me to call the sheriff's office before wasting my time in case the answer was no. I then called the sheriff's office to see if they would let me through, and just as David had predicted, the answer was a resounding NO.

The police knew that my dad had a vehicle and in their eyes that meant that he had a choice to either stay or evacuate like everyone else. I tried to go back to work, but the idea that my dad might be passed out on the floor of his house was turning my stomach to knots.

I decided that I would drive to the checkpoint and plead my case; maybe I'd run into some cops that would "look the other way," or maybe I could talk them into giving me a police escort, which I'd heard they were giving to residents of the area that had horses and livestock trapped behind the lines.

I spoke to David again just before I left; he offered to be my wingman, but I didn't take him up on it. We were both fairly certain that I wasn't going to get through the checkpoint, and I didn't want to waste his time. We used the rest of the conversation to discuss what I could do up at Ohana if I somehow managed to pull it off. He gave me a list of things that really needed to get done if I somehow made it home. I took off from the Secret Compass warehouse with my Nissan 4x4 pickup truck at around 11:30 a.m., praying that I'd be able to talk my way through the blockade.

* * *

The road around Horsetooth Reservoir was closed, so it took me about an hour to drive the long way down to Loveland and then double back through Masonville. This is the only way to access Masonville if the county road to Horsetooth Reservoir is closed. Anyone who knows the area knows what I mean. The detour finally brought me to the checkpoint below Buckhorn Canyon.

There was a cop parked at the intersection and when I got out of my truck and approached him, I could immediately sense that it wasn't going to go my way. I wasn't going to get a person listening to another person's persuasion, that much was clear. The cop radioed my request in and sure enough, the call went to the same sheriff's office, probably the same dispatcher. The answer was still a resounding NO. I asked if I could get a police escort to go in and check on my dad and the answer was still no. I walked back to my truck in frustration. I was really pissed off at having been told no and really pissed off that I had wasted an hour of my day, going around the river and through the woods to even get to the checkpoint, only to be told no again.

I stared at the cop and the smoke clouds billowing out of Buckhorn Canyon behind him, and seriously considered flooring it and weaving my way right around him. He wouldn't be able to leave his post and by the time they got somebody to answer the call, I'd be long gone. Besides, this cop couldn't shoot me for just wanting to go home, could he?

Then again, they might come arrest me after it was all said and done, two-three-four weeks later, since they had my license plate number and could easily identify who I was. The whole scenario was spinning me into an internal philosophical conflict that I have been unable to reconcile in recent years; the punk rock "F the cops" edict I grew up with, versus "some of your friends are in law enforcement now and they're doing good things." *C'mon, Cooper. Why don't you stop acting like an angry teenager?*

I have an old friend that spends the eight-plus hours in his day tracking down sexual predators and another friend advancing her career in forensics, what would they think of me if I charged past this cop car waving my middle finger? What would my community think of me if I got busted and was brought up on charges for evading law enforcement working a crisis? I sat there with the engine chugging in idle, thinking of all the work I had to do back at the warehouse and all the time I was wasting.

I slowly put the truck into reverse, turned around, and headed back toward Loveland. I didn't get very far before the rest of the punk rock edict, "F you, you can't tell me what to do" set in; I was barely thirty to forty seconds into my return trip before the gears in my head started turning.

What if I could find another way up the canyon? Was there a back way that I didn't know of? I immediately yanked the wheel and shot off the road, up the first driveway.

I spent the next ten minutes furiously charging up and down the county road's various offshoots, exploring, hoping for something, even driving through people's yards, but there was nothing. Back to the county road, back to Loveland.

I passed the entrance to the Bobcat Ridge trail system and didn't even bother checking it out, knowing all too well that Parks and Recreation had made sure long ago that even an ATV couldn't get onto the trails, let alone a full sized 4x4 vehicle.

I kept driving, getting more and more infuriated. Who the hell did the cops think they were, telling me I couldn't go home to get my dad? Or, anybody else for that matter? What authority did they have, telling a man who lived behind the fire lines that he couldn't go back to his home?

It wasn't like I was some tourist looky-loo…my home, my property, my freakin' dad, these were all giant question marks staring back at me and if I want to go tend to my home or my family, wasn't it my goddamned business if I wanted to take a risk in my life?

Yeah, but c'mon Shane, these guys are just doing what they're instructed to do, they're public servants that are there to protect the community. You can't go through life waving middle fingers at the cops.

Both trains of thought were swirling around in my head, competing to be my definitive philosophy. I felt like Gollum vs. Sméogol.

I kept driving, growing more and more restless with every dotted line on the pavement. Then, about two miles farther up the road, it came to me. I remembered that my dad and I had once visited a Seventh Day Adventist retreat/farm that was in the area, and their driveway was coming up on the right.

I made the turn and headed north into the valley, drawing pictures of the topography in my head. I already knew the driveway I was on was a dead end, but I had a feeling that if I could somehow continue driving north past the farm, I would eventually get back to the county road that went past Ohana, in an area about two miles north of the checkpoint. *If* I could make it back onto the county road after the checkpoint, I'd be home free.

It was all a question of what I could do once I hit the farm, which was a certain dead end in terms of a road. Once I got to the end of the driveway, I slowly maneuvered the truck through the last of the out buildings and houses. The farther I went, the more hopeless it got.

The valley to the north of the farm was completely sealed off with a waist-high barbed-wire fence, and there were no visible roads on the other side of it. The area was thick with bramble brush, trees, and tall grass.

I was about to give up all hope when I spied a lone gate. I quietly parked and had a closer look at the gate on foot, only to realize that it had a good-sized padlock on it. Of course. I wasn't about to go B&E, but then again, I was thinking to myself...*Man, how badly do I want to get home?????*

I scanned the houses to the left and right of the gate and started formulating a plan. It couldn't hurt to just ask. I walked up and knocked on the front door of one of the houses. The guy who answered didn't look overly suspicious or overly protective, so I immediately felt that I had a chance of at least appealing to him with my newfound mission.

I explained it all to this stranger; how I lived in the area,

how the fire was advancing, how I was just trying to get home
to check on my dad, how the cops wouldn't let me through the
checkpoint, and how I was hoping he would have a copy of the
key to the padlock on that damn gate? Please, mister? He broke
into a smile. I could see that he was game. He didn't have a key
to the gate, but he was willing to help.

"Just behind my house, the fence is down. If we put something
on the barbed wire, you can just hop the fence with your truck."

I stared at him in disbelief—I was so ecstatic to hear those
words come out of his mouth. We walked behind his house and
sure enough, there was a short section of the fence that had fallen
into disrepair. He had some scraps of plywood leftover from some
odd job and I used those to cover the barbed wire in two places,
about the same distance apart as my truck tires.

I ran back to my truck, hopped the curb up into his yard, and
then eased my truck up, onto, and over the pieces of plywood.
I waved fiercely at my newfound ally and flashed a thumbs-up
through the back window before scooting into the tall grass in
the valley north of the fence.

I paused for a minute to put the truck into four-wheel drive,
and then scanned the horizon ahead of me. The smoke from
the fire was billowing out of Buckhorn Canyon to the north, the
canyon where I lived, the canyon where I had spent three years
of my life building homes for my family.

I had no idea what was waiting for me, or if I could even
make it there. I glanced to my left and noticed that the grass in
front of the locked gate was just as tall as all the other grass. If
there had ever been a road in this valley, it was long gone.

My head began to churn…what if I got my truck stuck somewhere along the way, or what if I succeeded in getting home, only
to find our property on fire? What if the unthinkable became

reality? I simply had to make it back to Ohana to see it all for myself; I could not accept anything less.

The fact that I had made it over this fence without getting shot at or arrested was already one small victory in the journey back home, and with that in mind, I eased the truck into gear and proceeded north.

The sun was high above me as I plowed through the tall grass and sagebrush. I had absolutely no idea where I was going, except that I had to head north. The prairie was relatively flat and the truck powered through the foliage without any problems, until I ran into a configuration of irrigation ditches. Irrigation ditches are often dug along the boundary lines of a piece of property, to bring in water that can be shared by both landowners.

I knew better than to try anything head on or at high speed, especially with a stock truck. Everything on the Nissan is factory issued—no after market suspension, lifts, or anything like that. I've gotten in and out of some crazy places with the Nissan, but to do it with a stock truck, you've got to do it slow. Real slow.

I shifted into 4x4-low and crossed a couple of the irrigation ditches diagonally. Anyone who has ever off-roaded knows what I'm talking about. If you hit the ditch perpendicular or parallel, you end up with two wheels in the ditch at the same time and that can lead to you having to park your truck there until someone pulls you out.

I slowly and carefully eased the Nissan through the ditches one wheel at a time, checking traction with every tap of the gas and brake. That got me past the irrigation ditches and into a new section of the valley, which consisted of rolling hills and rock formations. I jumped out of the truck and climbed up one of the hills to survey the land ahead. I quickly realized that I was in a pinch, literally.

From the hill, I could see the Big Thompson water canal on my left. This canal is part of a massive water project designed to bring snowmelt from Rocky Mountain National Park down to the communities on the Front Range, starting with Horsetooth Reservoir and Fort Collins. This canal takes water from the Big Thompson River, which runs parallel to Highway 34 coming down from Estes Park, and then it turns north just outside of Loveland and heads over to the reservoir.

The canal runs parallel to the valley I was in, but I knew based on where it came out near Masonville that the canal *had* to eventually cut across the valley north of me in order to get to Masonville, to the east of where I stood, and that meant that if I wanted to continue north, I had to somehow get across this canal. There was simply no other way to continue going north.

The problem was that the bank was too steep to get my truck up onto it and even if I could, there were no bridges across the canal that were wide enough to support a vehicle, at least not from my vantage point. There was a single footbridge, and that was it. I had to consider abandoning the truck if I wanted to continue north, but I figured I would literally cross that bridge when I came to it. Pun intended.

I got back in the Nissan and navigated my way through a series of hills and ravines, all the while paying close attention to the steep bank holding in the canal on my left, until I spied a spot on the bank that was accessible. I eased up it with high hopes that new scenery might bring me a solution. I was wrong. No bridges of any kind, and I could see from the shift in the lay of the land ahead that the canal was going to drastically start to push east in a few hundred feet.

I quickly scanned the horizon to the east. The land on the other side of the ever-shrinking valley was too steep and besides, even if I could navigate it, I'd still have to cross the sonofabitch canal no matter what route I took.

My thoughts flashed to *The Dukes of Hazzard*…the Duke boys never gave a shit if a bridge was out, what the hell was I worrying about? Those crazy bastards started every show by jumping over a cop car to the tune of Waylon Jennings' theme song… "fighting the system like a true modern day Robin Hood…" Two or three times in every show, they'd gun it and just plow right through those rinky-dink signs, clearly indicating that the bridge was out, and then shoot the General Lee over what seemed like the width of the Mississippi River—and they didn't do it in slow motion like *Knight Rider*. In your face, awestruck early '80s kids watching TV.

I pictured myself taking a running start at the canal bank with the Nissan, and then suddenly recalled an article I had once read as a teenager, where *The Dukes of Hazzard* producers admitted destroying thirty to forty Dodge Chargers per season. *Seriously, Cooper? You're going to try and jump whaaaat? Shut up and get back in your truck.* Back to reality.

Once I quit daydreaming, I made up my mind I was going to exhaust all options with the truck before I abandoned it. Besides, the bank appeared to be wide enough for me to drive along the top of it, right next to the canal, at least until the terrain changed. Maybe there would be something along the canal's immediate push to the east, on the curve ahead.

With that in mind, I threw the truck back into gear and proceeded. I followed the bank a few hundred feet around the curve and presto…not only a bridge, but a bridge for vehicles! Victory! The journey could continue, at least for the time being.

I crossed the bridge and immediately discovered that the bank on the opposite side was actually a gravel road heading northeast along with the canal. After all that, a road. The county had built in access to monitor and maintain the canal.

I immediately stomped my foot on the gas and went tearing up the new-found road, realizing that I might still have to find a way to get off the wayward northeastern route and head true north, if the road didn't take me to where I wanted to go. I wasn't sure if it stuck with the canal or not, so I decided to follow it as far as I could.

I made note of a gate I passed, but kept going. After about half a mile, I slammed on the brakes as the road came to an abrupt end—a locked gate at the parking lot that provided access to the Bobcat Ridge Natural Area.

I spotted some official looking vehicles and official looking people in the parking lot that were gearing up for something important relating to the fire, but luckily they were so busy with what they were doing that they didn't see me, despite my grand entrance.

I slid down really low in my seat and eased the truck into reverse. I slowly backed up the road I had come down until I was out of the parking lot's line of sight, and then made a u-turn and headed back up to the gate I had passed.

I jumped out of the truck once again and dragged the gate open. That gave me access to new options heading north and a new set of downs. I squeezed through the gate with the truck and proceeded through a long meadow until I ran into the trail system that winds through the Bobcat Ridge Natural Area.

I continued driving on one of the trails until I came to an intersection of trails with a sign that indicated the various loops and their distances in miles. One marker referred to some kind of "Old Cabin" and the trail headed north, so I decided to follow that one. This seemed like it would be a breeze at the time;

my truck was wider than the trail, but I was able to stay on it by alternating back and forth between my left and right tires, in accordance with the obstacles that appeared. Little did I know what was ahead.

The first problem I ran into…another human. There were a couple of houses that backed up against the trail and I paused before continuing, wondering what the best approach might be. I finally decided to turn on my hazard blinkers, as if to give advance notice that I was having some sort of an emergency. I deliberately drove slowly in case the first house I passed was occupied.

Sure enough, a person appeared in the courtyard. The scowl on the face expressed a clear message of disapproval, so when the face plus body suddenly turned and bolted into the house, I floored it. In the United States, you just don't know. Maybe the guy was calling the police, or maybe he was going into his house to load up a firearm. I wasn't going to wait around to find out.

I bounced the Nissan around as many curves and over as many hills as I could, as quickly as I could, to put as much distance as possible between Sergeant Scowl and me. It all came to a screeching halt a mile or so later when the trail gave way to a steep ravine. There was a footbridge, clearly designed to transport hikers and cyclists cross the ravine, but it was no more than three feet wide and would not support my truck even if I could somehow magically shrink down its width.

The Duke boys and their "balancing on the two right wheels of the General Lee" heehawing came to mind, but I quickly shoved that out of my head. No more Duke boys. Or so it seemed. I jerked the wheel impulsively and headed down the first part of the embankment that seemed navigable before slamming on the brakes with both feet. I'm glad I did when I did or the truck might still be there.

The ravine dropped suddenly, about four to five feet, just beyond the bushes under my front bumper. This was a definite no-go and any man with any sense ought to know better than to rush in without scouting the terrain first. I was getting impatient with the mission and that was making careless.

I jumped out of the truck only to realize how completely screwed I was. There didn't seem to be any navigable means to cross the ravine other than the footbridge, which was already highlighted, circled, and underlined as a definitive NO with the truck.

I climbed back in and headed uphill due west, in a parallel line with the gully to see if I could find a crossing point. The farther I went, the steeper it all got, so I finally had to turn back in vain.

I drove back down the mountain and past the footbridge to see if there was anything east of what I'd seen so far. The ravine was steep on both sides, but I did come upon a point that was gradual enough on one side to have a look. Reality set in quickly…this would not be easy. I could get into the gully without too much effort, but getting out the other side or back the way I came in would be tough and that could spell certain doom for the truck.

Then it suddenly dawned on me that I had no water or medical supplies if I got hurt. What a freakin' genius. I began to cycle through the worst-case scenario ahead of me. There was no cell service, so I would not be able to call anyone for help if I needed it.

Also, every emergency vehicle in Larimer County was preoccupied with evacuating, fighting, and/or transporting people to and from the fire, so if I got the truck stuck, there was no way in hell I was going to get anyone to help me get it out anytime soon, especially behind the evacuation lines.

Let me get this straight, Cooper…no water, no food, no medical supplies,
no tools, no cell coverage, and no hope of getting anyone within a thousand
miles to help if anything goes wrong. Seriously, Cooper???
I briefly considered abandoning the truck right then and
there, but quickly changed my mind. It would take me hours and
hours to get home if I proceeded on foot.

I had to try and make it across the gully; it was a risk I would
have to take if I wanted to get home anytime soon and besides, I
reasoned I could always hike it if I got the Nissan stuck and had
no other choice, assuming that I didn't turn it over on myself.

I got back in the truck and carefully lowered it into the ravine.
I scanned my exit options to the left and to the right, and in a sudden fit of heavy metal fury that I can't even begin to explain…I
abruptly mashed the gas pedal to the floor. The truck gained speed
quickly as I plowed it downhill through the gully until I spied the
only spot that made sense, a lone section of the opposite embankment that wasn't loaded with rocks. It was a split-second decision.

I tightened my grip on the wheel and shot out of the ravine
with such force that the truck went airborne for what seemed like
a hundred years. It landed on its back wheels, and I bounced off
the ceiling onto the steering wheel as the truck floundered onto
its front wheels. I struggled to bring it all under control while
gasping for air in a desperate attempt to stop the vehicle from
overturning or going back over the edge.

It was all over in a matter of seconds, but with the wind
knocked out of me, it felt so much longer. In my blind determination to cross this damn ravine, I hadn't bothered to clip in
my seatbelt after the last scouting session and was now paying
the price for my lack of preparation. I sat there squawking like
a harpooned seal for a couple of minutes; luckily, other than my
pride, I wasn't hurt.

Once my breathing got back to normal, I spun the Nissan around and got back on the trail. After a couple more hills and valleys, I caught a glimpse of the "old cabin" in the distance and in a matter of minutes I was beside it. I didn't even bother stopping as I knew I still had a ways to go.

I dodged a couple of trees and proceeded north through the tall grass. I could sense by the lay of the land that the trail didn't stop at the cabin, but the thick foliage made it clear that no one had gone through it in years. My hunch was right. However faint, it was still a navigable trail.

I bounced the truck up a small hill until I came to a home-made gate made out of leftover fencing materials sewn together with bailing wire. It didn't look like it had been opened in years. I spent the next few minutes trying to undo the rusty bailing wire with my bare hands, and the next few minutes after that cursing myself once again for having forgotten to bring any tools. Then it dawned on me. I did bring a single, lone tool. A four thousand pound tool that I drove in myself.

I got back into the truck, inched it up to the gate, and tapped the gas pedal until the bailing wire snapped. After heaving the gate out of the way, I found myself on a gravel driveway.

Based on my knowledge of the land in the area, I had a feeling it was the long, curved driveway I had driven by a thousand times on the commute from my house to Fort Collins and back, a driveway that seemingly appeared out of nowhere from a hidden valley that came out on a ranch very close to the county road I was desperately trying to get back to. I hoped and prayed that I was right.

The quality of the driveway improved the farther I went, which could only mean that it was approaching a residence. Lo and behold…I sailed around the last curve and there it was, just

beyond a cluster of structures…the county road. I had surfaced
exactly where I had predicted I would, if I could make it through
the hidden valley I had just managed to navigate.

Great success! Or, so it seemed. I gunned it down the hill
around the last couple of curves and stomped on the brakes just
outside what appeared to be the main residence. I jumped out of
the truck and raised my voice to announce my presence.

"Hello?? Anybody there???"

My voice echoed off the cliffs surrounding the ranch. I turned
a slow 360 in what seemed like a scene out of a post apocalyptic
movie. I vividly remember how strange the sunlight looked and
felt; it reminded me of the science fiction movie *Pitch Black*, which
takes place on a hostile planet that has two suns.

The production team responsible for the cinematography in
this film pushed the lighting in the outdoor scenes to the point
where everything seems overexposed, as a means of conveying
what sunlight might look and feel like if it were generated by
two suns.

There I was, standing in the middle of what appeared to be
a vacant ranch, in 95-degree heat, and everything in view looked
and felt overexposed. It was so strange. I wonder if the adrenalin
coursing through my veins had anything to do with this.

"Hello???? Can anyone hear me???? Hello??????"

I kept it up for the next couple of minutes as I cautiously
made my way between the various structures. People that live
in the hills don't like trespassers and I didn't want to catch anyone off guard. Not surprisingly, the ranch was deserted—to be
expected with a mandatory evacuation. These people had cleared
out a long time ago. It didn't matter much to me, as I wasn't waiting around for tea and crumpets, but I didn't want to get shot.

Once I had determined that I was alone, I ran over to the

ranch's main gate to the county road. It was the last obstacle standing in the way of me getting home and all I had to do was swing it open and be on my way.

To my total dismay, I found it locked up tight with a hefty padlock. I couldn't believe it. I had come all this way only to hit a padlocked gate fifty feet from the county road. I could see the freakin' pavement through the fence, the pavement I just spent the last two hours trying to get back to. *Who the hell evacuates their ranch and padlocks their gate behind them? What if your goddamn house went up in flames, how are the firefighters supposed to get their trucks in there to put the fire out?*

Then it dawned on me. The gate was locked to deter looters from getting into the ranch while its occupants were evacuated; the firefighters would just break in if they came across structures on fire and had to gain access.

Well, if the firefighters could break in, then I sure as hell could break out. I began mentally preparing myself for a ramming of the gate, Mad Max style. The padlock would be no match for my truck, especially at thirty or forty miles an hour. I jumped into the Nissan and backed it up to the gravel driveway to give myself the sufficient runway I would need to get up to ramming speed.

I sat there for a moment to collect my thoughts before stomping on the gas. What if something unforeseen went wrong? What if I succeeded in smashing through the gate, only to have part of it take out my oil pan or puncture one of my tires? Then I'd be walking for the next ten miles. It always looked easy in the movies, but how would that translate in reality?

I was starting to doubt my plan. Plus, I was about to cause property damage on somebody else's ranch. How would I feel if I came home to property damage on mine? This would have been an easy call twenty years ago, but not so easy when you're a grown man with a family, a business, and a community that you care about.

Maybe I could come back at a later date and explain what happened, and reimburse them for their gate and lock? I wrestled with my thoughts just long enough to catch a glimpse of a second access gate to the ranch that ran along their fence line, close to the county road.

I quickly killed the ignition and ran over to inspect the new find. I was in luck, this gate was not locked, but I would have to cross a creek that ran through the ranch to get to this secondary gate, which was why the occupants didn't bother padlocking that one when they evacuated. The creek served as a natural barrier to their structures, and I would have to cross it to get off their property with my truck, if I didn't want to be Captain Caveman Gate Smasher.

I scouted the creek and the land around it for the next few minutes, until I found a possible solution. It wouldn't be easy, but considering everything else that I had been through in the last two hours, I wasn't about to back down from this challenge. It was going to take some work.

After fortifying the creek bank by removing and repositioning some of the stones, I carefully considered my next move. I would have to slowly lower the truck off the embankment at an angle to get it into the creek, one wheel at a time to keep it get from getting stuck. There were a lot of rocks and some good-sized boulders in the creek, but with the route I had planned, I felt that I had a good chance at getting across it.

Fortunately, the embankment on the opposite side of the creek wasn't very steep. If I could keep my momentum once I got moving, I would just have to maneuver my way around some bushes and small saplings on the other side once I got through the water.

I spent the next ten minutes rearranging various rocks to assist with getting the truck into the creek before crossing it on foot one last time to open the secondary gate in preparation for my departure. As I climbed back up the embankment on my return, I began to doubt my new plan.

What if I broke an axle, lowering the truck into the creek? What if I got it stuck in the creek, or on the opposite side? There'd be no way in hell I could get anyone to help me get it out any time soon, that much was already crystal clear. Not only would I be walking for the next ten miles, but that might also mean parting ways with the Nissan, once and for all.

I tried to imagine the looks on the faces of the people who owned the ranch once they returned from the evacuation, only to find somebody's truck jammed into the creek that ran through their property.

What was I going to do, leave a note? "So uh, yeah, dipshit trespasser here, I swear I wasn't looting, please give me a call at this number and I'll come get my vehicle." Yeah, right. I'd be just as likely to get a call to come check out the bonfire-formerly-known-as-a-1991-Nissan-pickup. I sat on a rock at the edge of the embankment for a few minutes, unsure of what to do next.

For the love of everything holy, Cooper—why do you have to be so freakin' difficult? Ram the truck through the goddamn gate and be done with it, who gives a shit?? You can come back later and pay them back for their gate, or anonymously send them a check, whatever. The alternative means getting the truck stuck and not making it home, why would you take that chance?

The delirium had me pinned. I couldn't make up my mind what to do. Both plans had their pros and cons. I finally decided once and for all that I didn't want to be Captain Caveman Gate

Smasher so that left me only one other choice. I slowly walked back to the Nissan and fired it up.

I took the video camera I had sitting in the shotgun seat out of its bag and wondered if it might be cool to videotape what I was about to do. I'd either have proof that I was a total lunatic or, on the other hand, proof that I got the truck stuck in a creek, highlighted by the fact that I had tried it one-handed, and that I had made the wrong final choice on how to get home. Not to mention that I also would have indisputable evidence of whatever laws I had broken, in case the cops wanted to arrest me for breaking and entering, trespassing, and/or suspected looting. I put the camera back in the bag.

If I had any hope of succeeding at getting off this ranch, I would need to have both hands on the wheel. That would be the last thing in the world I wanted to face—having to explain to my family and friends that I almost got home, but I didn't make it because I tried to do it with one hand on the steering wheel and one hand videotaping myself.

I'd get the Horse's Ass Award for sure, and perhaps a Lifetime Achievement wreath to go along with it. *Last call, Cooper. What's it gonna be? Ram the gate or ford the creek?*

I put the truck into 4x4-low and maneuvered it over to the edge of the creek. With extreme caution, I gradually lowered the left front tire off the embankment, inch by inch. The front axle scraped against the rocks beneath the Nissan as I eased it forward until the left rear tire fell into the creek as well. I was past the point of no return.

The truck lurched and listed heavily to one side, like it was going to turn over. I knew I was in danger of flipping the vehicle so instinctively I threw as much of my body weight as I could into the shotgun seat without letting go of the steering wheel with my left hand. I grabbed the handle above the shotgun seat with my right hand and hung there for a few seconds, swaying back and forth in a crude attempt to measure the overall balance of the truck.

It seemed steady, but I couldn't predict what was going to happen next and I was afraid to sit back down in the driver's seat. I was pretty sure that if I could just get the other front tire into the creek, the truck would naturally right itself. It was just a matter of a few more feet.

I realized that I was still able to reach the gas pedal with my left foot, despite the fact that I was hanging there like a chimp. It quickly dawned on me that I didn't have to be in the driver's seat to actually drive. *Okay, let's see if I can pull this off.*

I shifted as much of my body weight as I could to the right side of the truck, while blindly feeling for the accelerator with my left toe. Once I found it, I gently tapped on the gas while making slight adjustments to the steering wheel with my left hand, until the right front tire plopped off the edge of the embankment. Instantly, the truck righted itself.

I got back into the driver's seat and paused for a minute to wipe the sweat off my brow. *Man, this is some crazy shit.* I let gravity do most of the work in getting the last tire off the embankment by pressing and releasing the brake until the entire truck was in the creek. I went back to the accelerator and slowly eased the Nissan around the biggest of the boulders until I had a clear shot at the opposite creek bank. It was the last remaining obstacle that stood in the way of me going home.

I gritted my teeth and stomped on the gas. The Nissan tore through the rest of the creek and up onto the embankment, but it began to lose traction in the mud. I started screaming as the truck slid sideways and slowed to a crawl instead of continuing forward.

"C'MON!!!!!!!!!!!!!!!!!!"

I furiously yanked the wheel to redirect the slide off the mud, and then mashed the gas pedal to the floor as soon as I hit rock again. The truck heaved as it regained traction and plowed up the embankment.

My original intention was to go around the bushes and trees, but given the circumstances, I didn't have a choice. I didn't want to lose it in the creek and I simply could not risk giving up any more momentum.

With that in mind, I mowed my way up and over the shrubs and saplings, screaming like I was being murdered in the middle of the night. Suddenly, I was home free. I began pounding my fist against the door on the outside of the truck, hooting and hollering at the top of my lungs as I plowed through the remaining foliage.

In an instant, I floored the Nissan through the secondary gate and up onto the asphalt. My tires squealed as I caught pavement and shot up the county road in the direction of Ohana.

* * *

I don't remember much about the first few minutes of driving once I got back onto the pavement. I wonder if bouncing off the ceiling of the truck earlier in the trip had jostled my brain, or if the adrenalin blast I got from the creek crossing had temporarily fried my circuits. I do recall careening around every corner like a bat out of hell, but the first part of my drive up the county road seems like a blur to me now.

I remember coming over the first major hill; you get a broad view of the valley above the canyon that Ohana sits in, once you get to the top. I couldn't believe how much smoke was billowing out of the canyon. From below, it looked like everything in our beloved valley had gone up in flames.

I clenched my hands tightly around the steering wheel and continued driving as fast as I could. My fear of what I might find was eating me alive. I didn't know if we had lost it all, lost some, or lost nothing, or if my dad was alive or dead.

Just before the "narrows" (a tight, winding section of Buckhorn Canyon), I spied a government vehicle approaching in the oncoming lane. The occupant began slowing to a stop as soon as he caught sight of my truck, as if to suggest that I should do the same, as if we were going to have some sort of a discussion.

I jammed the accelerator to the floor and blew right past him. He took both hands off the wheel momentarily to vigorously shrug at me, like he couldn't believe that I wasn't going to stop. I grimaced as I passed him, determined more than ever to get home. No one was going to stop me. They would've had to bring in tanks to stop me from going home.

I maneuvered the truck through the various hairpin turns in the narrows and popped out on the other side, just below Ohana. The smoke was so thick that I could barely see. My palms were sweating hard as I sailed around the last curve and shot off the country road onto our driveway. The trees to my immediate left and right weren't on fire, which in itself was amazing. I wanted to get out and kiss each and every one of them.

I was so fixated with seeing it all for myself as quickly as possible that I nearly lost control of the truck as I blasted up the driveway. My heart was beating a thousand miles an hour. It would only be a matter of thirty to forty seconds before I made the climb to my dad's house at the top of the ranch, and then I would have all the answers.

The anticipation was bubbling in my stomach like lava. I came to the fork in the driveway and shot up the left leg. So far, so good. None of the structures on our property that I could see had sustained any damage. I careened around the last turn above my house and slammed on the brakes just outside my dad's place. The reality of the situation set in quickly as I grabbed the video camera and jumped out of the truck.

I stared out over the valley...I couldn't believe my eyes. It was a total war zone, like a scene out of a movie. The entire mountain directly to the north of Ohana was on fire. The flames had already jumped a huge section of orange retardant that had been sprayed and were close to structures, but as far as I could tell, none of our neighbors had lost anything.

There were water tankers set up outside the seven homes at the base of the mountain, accompanied by seventy to eighty firefighters battling the blaze in various capacities. A few bulldozers had been brought in to build an access road across the base of the mountain, and the firefighters were using that road to get crews in to dig ditches that would serve as firebreaks.

There was a full helicopter refueling station set up in our neighbor's yard—our immediate neighbor due northwest. The blaze had burned down to the county road in at least one spot to within a hundred feet of our property, but amazingly enough, it had not jumped the road and nothing on our ranch had caught fire. Ohana had been spared, at least for the time being.

I ran over and pounded on my dad's door before trying the knob, which turned freely in my hand. I threw open the door and there was my dad, sitting on his couch. He stared at me in disbelief for a couple of seconds before getting up to greet me. I raced over to him and threw my arms around him.

"Man, you don't know what kind of crazy shit I did to get here, Dad."

I proceeded to tell him the saga of how I had gotten past the checkpoint and the two-hour ordeal that I went through, just to get home. He confirmed in the conversation that followed that we had in fact lost power at the ranch. I was really happy to see him, but also frustrated that he had not simply gotten into his truck and evacuated once they cut the power. He had to have known that I would be worried sick if I couldn't communicate with him. I wasn't about to get into an argument about it, as we had been through all of that the previous summer, when we were all supposed to evacuate from the Crystal Mountain Fire and he had refused to leave. It was going to be tricky to get him to leave this time around, but I figured that he'd be more likely to go since there was no power.

Nevertheless, I had to choose my words carefully. If I went frontal assault and started yelling, he would batten down the hatches and that would be the end of any hope of getting him to come with me when I left.

"Look, Dad…I can't communicate with you any more and it'll drive me crazy if I don't know that you're safe. If anything happens to you, you won't be able to call for help. Plus, there's no power and no water, you can't cook or take a shower. C'mon Dad, it's time to go."

Do you know what his answer was? Without even blinking, the old man from Brooklyn looked me straight in the face and said: "I can boil water."

I couldn't believe it. *Seriously, you stubborn mule? You're going to schlep water to and from the lake and boil it???* I didn't let his answer faze me or blow me off course. Eye on the prize, and the prize was getting him to leave with me.

"Yeah, Dad, I know you could do that, but why would you?"

I proceeded to explain to him that I had communicated with the insurance company that held our policies and they would be paying for our accommodations while we were displaced. He paused to think about it, which meant that I had a real chance at getting him to finally evacuate. Then it dawned me, a chance to seal the deal.

"Listen, Dad, I can't drive out of here. If I try and drive past the checkpoint with my truck, the cops will recognize me in a heartbeat because I met them face-to-face and tried to talk my way up here before going renegade. I will get arrested if I try and leave by myself. The only way I can get outta here is to vacate in your truck. And you have to drive."

My dad finally concurred and he agreed to drive, so we made a plan. I had about an hour's worth of work I had to get done up at Ohana and that meant that he'd have a little time to pack and gather his things.

I ran out of the house and was about to get back into my truck when suddenly, with a deafening clatter, a helicopter appeared right above me. It came over my dad's house and couldn't have been more than two hundred feet off the ground. I immediately turned on the video camera and captured what was about to happen next.

The chopper was an Erickson S-64 Air Crane Helitanker, designed to combat wildfires. I watched in awe as it swooped down to the lake just below my house and began to suck up water through a giant snorkel (see photo 4). Within ten seconds, it sucked up more than two thousand gallons and then took off in the direction of the mountains across the road. It dumped its payload on the tallest flames and then returned along the same flight path for more water.

I could tell by the water level in the lake that the firefighters had been working it for a while; about a fourth of it was gone. They could have gone right ahead and drained every last drop, for all I cared. Coming home to an empty lake sure sounded far better than coming home to no house and every minute that the fire raged a hundred feet from our property was another minute that the flames could jump the road and ravage Ohana. I hoped and prayed that there would be enough water in the lake to beat back the inferno before it could eat up any more structures.

I made my way down to the valley, which was dangerously close to the flames. I managed to take a few pictures and I included one of them in this book, showing our barn and the mountain to the north behind it (see back cover).

I stopped at my wife's parents' house first on my errand list, to get their extra freezer plugged into their generator. When we built our houses, David and Lisa spent the extra money to install a propane generator that would kick on automatically if the power went out, which can happen from time to time when you're living in a rural setting.

However, the generator was designed to provide electricity to only a few outlets in his house, namely the kitchen outlets, which kept their refrigerator going, but not their freezer, which was in the garage.

The freezers we have at Ohana store most of the food we grow and harvest in the garden, and to lose even one freezer's contents means a significant loss of food that takes months to grow and care for. Luckily, David and Lisa's freezer had only gone a few hours without power, so the food was still frozen.

As David had instructed, I ran an extension cord from one of the kitchen outlets into the garage and plugged in the freezer. I gathered a few personal items, watered the plants, and made my way to the garden.

The loss of electrical power meant that the pumps in the wells would not run, but there was still two thousand gallons in our cistern up on the hill. All structures below the cistern would have gravity-fed running water until the cistern ran dry.

The garden is set up with an automated sprinkler system that runs on electricity, so until power came back on, the garden would not get watered. I connected all the spare hoses together, and after connecting to the spigot, I hand watered most of the garden.

I then made my way to the chicken coop. We had just finished building it, a few weeks previously. I filled every receptacle I could find with water, including a small wagon, and dumped whatever birdseed was left in the bins onto the ground.

I considered leaving the gate to the coop ajar so the chickens could escape if the structure caught fire, but then quickly realized that they wouldn't make it through the night if a fox or skunk found their way into the coop.

I bolted the gate and headed for the cabins, where we were storing extra food for the yoga retreat and summertime family get-togethers. One by one, I cleared out all the refrigerators and freezers. From the valley, I drove back up to my house and took care of business there.

I went out on the deck for a split second just as four planes whizzed by. They all bombed one of the houses on the mountain across the street with orange flame retardant, one after another. The flames were dangerously close to that house. I could tell from an orange line that ran higher on the mountain that the first attempt to beat back the flames with the retardant had failed.

I gathered up some clothes and a few personal effects and then drove back up to my dad's place. We transferred everything out of my truck into his truck and then arranged to leave. As we made our way off the ranch, I noticed that the firefighters had paid Ohana a visit while we were gone.

I could see that they had removed all the lawn furniture in

and around our homes and piled it up in our yards. A few of the trees near structures had all of their lower limbs removed, and the grass around all of our propane tanks had been cut back. That could only mean one thing...the firefighters had prepared our ranch in case the fire jumped the road and made it onto our property. It made my stomach turn just thinking about it. I stared at the side view mirror as Ohana faded away in the distance, hoping that it would still be there when my family and I returned. It was heartache that I cannot properly put into words, even today.

My dad and I drove in near silence until we came to the last straightaway into Masonville. I crawled under some tarps in the extended cab of my dad's truck when we arrived at the checkpoint, in case the police stopped us for an extended period of time. Fortunately, they were not stopping vehicles coming out of the evacuation zone and we were able to make our way to Fort Collins without any further delays.

* * *

I tried to explain it all to my wife that evening as we were on our way to the hotel, but it seemed like I was paraphrasing a story she had already heard. My own story, in fact, one I had written myself. In 2009, I published a science fiction novel titled *Aktiya: The Ignition Sequence* and three of the main characters in this story spend a significant amount of time off-roading with a 4x4 vehicle in the Cascade Mountains.

I can't say there is a lot in common between the fictional novel I wrote in 2009 and the non-fictional backcountry journey I took to get back home, but it still felt weird to try to explain it all to someone that had read *Aktiya* without sounding like I was ripping myself off.

Rachel just shook her head as I recalled some of the more harrowing details. I'm grateful that she tolerates the crazy things I do sometimes.

Anyway, after successfully retrieving my dad from the hills, it was pretty obvious that we weren't all going to sleep in the Secret Compass warehouse together. Rachel had gone long enough without easy access to bathing and laundry facilities and just as I had promised my dad before we left Ohana, as soon as we got back to town, I would make preparations for all of us to spend the remainder of the evacuation in a hotel.

Considering that the High Park Fire had already displaced thousands of people, it was tough to find a hotel in Larimer County that had accommodations for any extended period of time, but we did manage to secure two rooms for the next three nights. After getting something to eat, we checked in around 8:00 p.m. I was really tired after the rough ride back to Ohana and all I really wanted to do was take a shower and pass out.

Then, it hit me all at once. I checked the calendar on my phone just to make sure and I still couldn't believe it. I stared at Rachel in the reflection of the bathroom mirror and slowly put my arm around her.

"Happy Anniversary, sweetie."

She just stared at me in disbelief. We had tied the knot exactly eight years ago, on June 12th, 2004, and with everything that had happened over the past week, we had gotten so wrapped up in the stress of it all that we had both simultaneously forgotten our own wedding anniversary. Neither one of us had done any planning, made any reservations at any restaurants, or bought any gifts.

It was a sad state of affairs for two happily married people to realize that they were so stressed out that they had overlooked one of the most important days of the year. I'm pretty sure that Rachel started crying.

We spent the next few minutes frantically trying to set up a last minute plan for an impromptu celebration. Some of our closest friends were game; we succeeded in getting a handful of people to meet us out for drinks since dinner had already come and gone. We arranged for Ben to sleep in my dad's hotel room in order to get some alone time in our room once we got back from the night ahead of us, and then set out on foot in the direction of the nearest bar.

We met up with our friends at the Sundance Steakhouse and Saloon on Mulberry Street. It was the closest watering hole to our hotel and it was also pretty close to the neighborhood where our friends lived so they wouldn't have to drive home after getting plastered with us.

The Sundance has a hefty cover charge for live music and I blew close to a hundred dollars in like thirty seconds; thankfully the drink specials that came with the entry were cheap. It was one of those places that gives away beers and wells for a nickel or something, until like 10:00 p.m. You're so hammered on cheap drinks that by the time the special ends, you don't care if the same beers and wells magically become six dollars apiece. Brilliant plan if you're running a bar.

We proceeded to get rip roaring drunk over the next few hours and I'm pretty sure we closed the bar. It was a fun night and I'm really grateful that our friends were able to make it out on such short notice.

Rachel and I stumbled back to our hotel and just as we were about to head upstairs, a figure emerged from the shadows. It was a man dressed in heavy clothing. He looked bewildered, like he was in some kind of shock. His face was strangely familiar and after staring at him for a few seconds, it came to me.

Every year, the mountain communities living in Rist Canyon and Buckhorn Canyon meet up at Ohana for our annual trash cleanup. Believe it or not, people still throw beer cans out of their car windows on country drives in this day and age, and unless the residents living in the country want to live in an accumulating pile of litter, somebody has to clean all that up. We comb up and down the canyons once a year, bagging up all sorts of crap we find on the edges of the road, and then head back to Ohana for a barbeque when we're done. We've been doing it for years.

The man standing in front of Rachel and me was a man we had just met at the beginning of May, not two months earlier. He lived in Rist Canyon and he was one of the Rist Canyon Volunteer Firefighters. I'll call him Tom, to protect his identity. There we were, standing face to face with a firefighter that we knew, in front of a hotel in Fort Collins, at two in the morning. He was blackened from head to toe and he just stood there, staring at us.

Like I said, I think he was in some kind of shock. Once he recognized who we were, he literally burst into tears. I lurched forward and wrapped my arms around him with such force that I cut my hand open on one of the tools hanging off his backpack.

He had just come back to town after six straight days of fighting on the front lines of the inferno raging in our beloved mountain community, only to find that all the hotels were booked up. There was no place for this man to put his head down and get some rest.

The next few minutes were a blur as we tried to console him. The fire had claimed many homes on that very night and he was beside himself with heartache and grief. We absolutely insisted that Tom take the remaining bed in our hotel room and we weren't going to take no for an answer. It would have been nice to spend our anniversary night alone, but considering the circumstances, we were quick to shelve our own personal expectations and needs. After serious persistence, he finally accepted our offer.

I helped him get all his gear into our room and he then spent the next fifteen minutes in the shower. That gave me a chance to patch up my hand. After Tom got cleaned up, he gave Rachel and I the grim news.

The High Park Fire had roared right through Rist Canyon, leaving little in its wake. Entire communities like Stratton Park and Whale Rock were incinerated. The houses that the firefighters had been able to save were few and far between. Even with the recent influx of federally provided manpower and equipment, they were losing structures by the minute and the crews were overwhelmed.

On almost all fronts, the fire was growing with such force that it would be impossible to extinguish or even contain in the days and weeks ahead without major reinforcements. Tom struggled to hold back tears as he recounted some of the battles that the Rist Canyon Volunteer Fire Department had fought over the past few days and nights.

I tried my best to reassure him that the community stood behind the firefighters, and certainly they had not worked so hard for nothing. The real count was the homes saved, not the homes lost. Besides, the firefighters had saved other peoples' homes while their own homes burned down.

Tom was so delirious from lack of sleep that he began to nod off while he was talking to us. We called it a night, but not ten minutes into what could have been the first real night of sleep for this man in more than a week, his radio lit up. More structures were on fire and they needed him back on the front lines. I couldn't believe what was happening as I watched an exhausted firefighter put his blackened suit back on, shoulder his pack full of tools, and head back out into the night.

I tried to get back to sleep once he was gone, but I just couldn't. I'm more sensitive than I like to let on and considering the weight of June 12th, my head was in a state of total disarray. I didn't want to admit it, but the extreme range of emotions that the evacuation had bagged up and handed to me was wearing me down.

Just within the last sixteen hours alone...the fear of losing my dad and/or our property, the adrenalin-laced euphoria of successfully circumventing the roadblocks and making it home, the disappointment in myself for the forgotten anniversary, the raging highs of getting hammered with my friends, the heartache of meeting Tom and hearing the truth from the frontlines of the inferno...all packed into the last sixteen hours. It was enough to make a man crack.

I kept tossing and turning. I was having a hard time process-ing the losses that the community was sustaining; my thoughts kept returning to the anguish and hopelessness the local firefight-ers like Tom must be feeling.

I couldn't imagine what it felt like to watch your beloved com-munity get ravaged by a demon that's a hundred times stronger and faster than you, your team, and all your equipment; a demon with seemingly limitless power to keep growing and growing with no end in sight.

It had to be absolutely maddening to be part of a fire depart-ment for years on end, dedicated to protecting the homes of your neighbors and friends, only to watch them go up in flames one by one as you fought your ass off each step of the way, day and night. These are the bravest men and women in our society and it hurt so much to think of how the situation was affecting them. God Almighty.

I began to wonder if the community would or could ever recover from such a nightmare. I fell into the despair of it, pondering the fates of all those souls that were happy prior to June 9th, and where they'd end up when the ash settled onto the wasteland formerly known as their community.

The firefighters had saved Stove Prairie Elementary School, the school that my son Ben attended, but what kids would be left to go to the school if everyone's houses burned down? Would this be the end of life in the mountain community as we knew it? The unknown future was eating me alive. I kept tossing and turning.

Suddenly, my cell phone rang. *Who could be calling me so late?* I hurriedly yanked my phone out my pocket and bolted into the bathroom to avoid having it wake up my wife. I strained to get my eyes to focus on the screen in the vanity's blaring lights.

It was Allen, my old friend from the HeadCrash days. I couldn't believe it. Of all the people to call me up at a moment when I was teetering at the edge of darkness, at the end of one of the craziest days of my life, it was Allen. This was a friend that gave me my first real chance in life, at a time when I was barely a man and a sputtering, struggling, lost man at that.

I question whether I would have made it anywhere as a front man in any of the bands I was in, whether I would have written any books, whether I would have built any houses, or started any companies if it hadn't been for Allen, giving me that first shot at doing something great, way back in 1993.

Of all the people on this earth that could make me laugh and forget my troubles, of all the people in the world that could give me temporary reprieve, it was Allen. Through thick and thin, through all that was gained and all that was lost with the band, our friendship had persevered.

Allen had seen the news and he was calling all the way from Germany to check in on my family. My head was spinning from all the drinks I had downed at the saloon earlier in the night and I was exhausted from everything that had happened in the last sixteen hours, but of course I was thrilled that he had called. His timing was beyond coincidence and exactly what I needed.

I spent the next ten minutes getting him brought up to speed with the latest news from the fire and then the next forty-five minutes laughing at some of the hilarious things that happened to us along the way.

Any time I ever talk to Allen, no matter how the conversation starts, we end up rehashing one or more of the crazy situations we found ourselves in back in K-Town and on the road with the band. It was just what the doctor ordered at the end of June 12th, 2012—getting taken back to yesteryear, if only for a brief moment, to help me temporarily forget my troubles.

An hour later, I finally climbed back into bed, my head flooded with fresh memories of happier times. What a way to end one of the craziest days of my life. I fell asleep before the reality of my situation had a chance to creep back in.

SIX

Dissention

The days and nights got bleaker and bleaker as they came and went. A week into it, the High Park Fire was zero percent contained and growing exponentially. It was out of control with no hope of containment in the near future.

The smoke was so thick one night in Fort Collins that people were having a hard time breathing, even indoors. Meanwhile, the temperature soared into the hundreds, combined with gusty winds at high elevations. We were in the opening stages of a record-breaking heat wave and because of the persistent hot and dry conditions—day in and day out—the firefighters combating the inferno couldn't get a break.

Citizens living behind the fire lines were told to prepare for the worst, if and when they got to go home. It was clear that we would not be going home in the near future, if at all. Our family had no choice but to settle into what appeared to be an indefinite evacuation.

We began to recognize in that first week how acclimated we had gotten to our secluded life in the mountains over the last seven years and how strange it felt to live in town again. It didn't take me long to realize how much I despised the traffic, the noise, and the heat.

Ohana sits at 6,700 feet elevation and is always five to ten degrees cooler in the summertime during the day. At night, the temperature difference is even more pronounced. At home, it gets to the low sixties at night, but in Fort Collins, with all that concrete and asphalt soaking up the heat during the day, the temperature doesn't ever seem to want to go down at night.

I do not like air conditioning, but with the evacuation, I didn't have a choice. I had to use it because it was just too hot to go without it. I found myself growing more and more disgusted with the heat, the traffic, and the stress that came with living in town again.

I spent most of my time at the shop, trying to keep up with Secret Compass business and Rachel spent most of her time attending evacuee meetings. There were meetings held every day for people displaced by the High Park Fire, and they were not going well. There was a growing sense of frustration over the lack of information coming in from behind the burn lines, in terms of which homes had been lost and which homes had been spared.

There were instances where the fire department was wrong on both sides of the equation. Some folks were told their home had burned down, only to get conflicting information elsewhere, and other folks were told their home had survived, only to find out later that it actually had not. Most people simply didn't know whether their houses had made it or not for days on end and were out of the minds with grief and anxiety over it.

The firefighters were overwhelmed and they couldn't be

blamed for not having accurate information in real time, on what had been saved and what had been lost, especially because the blaze kept popping back up in places where it had already been extinguished.

There were instances where firefighters were coming back to the put out flames on the same houses, over and over again. Hundreds of structures had burned down, but it wasn't clear which structures. The lack of accurate information became a huge problem.

There were a growing number of angry residents that demanded to be allowed past the barricades to check on their property, but because of the soaring temperatures and high winds, the blaze was unpredictable and as a result, the local police were ordered to enforce the checkpoints.

There were reports of people charging past the barricades in their pickups. Before the situation got out of hand, the county called in the National Guard to relieve the police officers on duty. The National Guard set up generators, armed guards, and floodlights at checkpoints on all the roads going to and from the burn area, and that made it clear that no one else was getting in, residents or not. No exceptions.

That was followed by a huge spike in the local sales of telescopes, binoculars, and even hunting scopes, as residents rushed to get whatever tools they could to help them learn the fate of their homes. Some turned to satellite imagery, but in many cases, the data was days to weeks old, and was therefore not an accurate assessment.

The evening news was an endless series of people with tears streaming down their faces and an overwhelming purveyor of anxiety. Collectively, the stress was tearing the community apart.

In the wake of the disaster, our family was left scrambling

for not only our own immediate needs, but also the immediate needs of our friends in the yoga retreat that were also forced to leave Ohana when we evacuated. We had seventeen guests to look after—most of them out-of-town guests—that simply had no place to go. They were determined to carry on with the yoga course, despite the emergency.

We arranged for temporary quarters, but when it was clear that the temporary quarters would no longer suffice, our family arranged to have the retreat continue at a friend's meditation studio in Fort Collins. Rachel and I hustled to provide our guests with essentials, such as bedding, pillows, and towels.

Despite our efforts, the accommodations were crowded and a far cry from the original plan back at Ohana, and within a few days, the course began to fall apart. The friend who owned the meditation studio called one night to report that someone had stolen $500 in cash from her bedroom above the studio. She wanted the entire yoga retreat out of her quarters by morning, and we had to oblige.

Our family was left trying to sort out places for seventeen guests to stay on a moment's notice, when we weren't even sure if we had places to stay ourselves. As if there wasn't enough stress. In the end, the yoga retreat was moved to a ranch north of Loveland that hadn't been evacuated, at least for the time being.

By the weekend, Rachel and I were forced to vacate our hotel to make way for guests that had already booked our rooms in advance. We packed up Ben and my dad and started to make our way toward Raymond, Colorado. The plan was that we would all attend a Father's Day celebration with some family that owned a cabin in the mountains, but I never made it there. I never even made it out of Fort Collins that morning.

Following an unpleasant exchange of words with my wife, I

abruptly pulled the car off the road while we were still in town and in a monumental lapse of judgment, I got out and started walking in the opposite direction.

The lack of sleep, the stress, and anxiety over the past week had taken its toll and I wasn't thinking clearly, to say the least. I walked furiously, but aimlessly. I didn't know where I was going and I didn't have a plan. I just knew that my head felt like it was going to explode and I reasoned that if I kept putting one foot in front of the other, my head just might be spared.

At one point, I sat down in the doorway of one of the local businesses at the edge of town and actually fell asleep with my head in my lap. I woke up just as troubled as I was when I had fallen asleep. I tried to think clearly, but I just couldn't. A wide variety of options came to mind, most of them involving fleeing the crisis and airplanes that could help me do it.

I considered taking a shuttle to Denver International Airport and then taking a flight back to Germany with nothing more than the clothes I was wearing. I then considered a flight to a variety of other destinations, anywhere-but-here, with nothing more than the clothes I was wearing.

I got up and kept walking in the direction of the Secret Compass warehouse. I tried to convince the cyclone blowing through my mind to cut me some slack, but it was too powerful. Once I got to the warehouse, I promptly got into my car and drove out onto I-25, heading south in the direction of the airport. Gradually, I was able to force a little light in around the edges. It made all the difference in the world.

As the storm in my head started to ease up, I came to the conclusion that if I woke up in another country, or even another state, I would end up regretting my decision. I couldn't just abandon Rachel, Ben, or my dad, but I also had to recognize that I was at the end of my rope. I simply could not stay in Fort Collins, for my own personal sanity.

I directed my car off the interstate onto Highway 34 in the direction of Estes Park. This is a remote town that's about an hour from Fort Collins, way up in the mountains. It sits atop a winding canyon at the edge of Rocky Mountain National Park. The farther up the canyon I drove, the more I realized how badly the stress and anxiety were affecting me. I nearly fell asleep two or three times along the way, one time just as I was drifting into oncoming traffic. Their horns blasted me awake. I instinctively overcorrected to avoid having a head-on collision, and then fought like a madman to keep my car from launching into the Big Thompson River on the other side of the road. I think the 360-degree skid marks on the pavement may still be there. Somehow, someway, I missed everything and everything moving missed me.

Seconds later I pulled off the road to a stop and instantly broke into a cold sweat. The air stunk of burned tires and my own B.O. I dozed for a few minutes to take the edge off, and then pressed on. I was determined to make it to Estes Park, and half an hour later I finally pulled into town.

The giant cloud of smoke sitting over Fort Collins in the distance reminded me of why I left in the first place. I got a room at the first motel I could find and fell asleep face first on the bed with my shoes on.

* * *

I awoke at dusk, after having slept for six or seven hours. I can't remember the last time I had slept so long during the day. It had to have been back in the band days when I didn't have anything to do but party my ass off and play shows. Nowadays, it seems as if every second of every waking hour has something jammed into it and it's been like that for years. I'm hoping that it'll all slow down, one day. Anyhow, the sleep did me good. I awoke with a renewed sense of clarity, and since my grasp on clarity seemed to be getting more and more elusive the further we got into the evacuation, I had to make the most use of it when I had it.

I called my wife and apologized for my erratic behavior. We both agreed that the stress in Fort Collins was unbearable and that the change of scenery up in Estes Park might do us both good. I then called my dad and spoke with him. He had gotten a good rate on a motel in Loveland, and he was prepared to wait out the evacuation there. After apologizing to him, I called Rachel's dad and apologized to him as well, for my behavior. I did everything I could to reassure him that I was doing my best to keep it together, for the sake of his daughter and the well being of our family.

It was good to talk to my dad and Rachel's dad. It's important to me that the dads have faith in me. They have both seen me through a tremendous amount of stress along the way and it would render everything I have accomplished as meaningless if I fell apart when the going got tough.

Once I got off the phone, I went and got something to eat and then headed back to the motel. I was comforted by the fact that my wife and son would be in Estes Park in the morning and together Rachel and I could make a plan for the next week or so. I was going to push for us to stay in Estes until the evacuation was over. The stress back in our hometown was unbearable. I fell back asleep for another nine hours, and it felt like the best sleep I had gotten in years.

It was great to see Rachel and Ben the following morning. I wrapped my arms around them and squeezed them tight like

they were the last two people on Earth. The sun was rising on a
new day and what felt like a fresh start.

We went and got some breakfast at a local restaurant and
when it was time to settle up, the manager came by and told us
that we didn't have to pay. The small talk we had made with the
waitress about being evacuated had made its way up to her boss
and he comped our meals. We were pleasantly shocked and of
course very grateful.

If I haven't said it before, I'll say it now: the outpouring of
support from our community during this crisis was amazing. This
comped breakfast was just one of many examples of the human
kindness our family encountered in the time we spent evacuated
from our homes.

Jax, one of my favorite restaurants in Fort Collins, fed *all*
evacuees, anyone forced from their home by the fire, for free
during the first week of the evacuation. They were not the only
restaurant or business that gave back to our community in its
time of need.

After breakfast, I checked in with our insurance agent to make
sure we would still be covered on our out-of-pocket expenses if
we chose to stay in Estes Park rather than Fort Collins while we
were displaced. Once I got the green light, we set out to find a
place to stay for the next few days.

We ended up at a hotel that was right by a creek that ran
through the town, and we were lucky enough to get a room that
faced the water. If you left the door to the balcony ajar, you could
hear the creek from our room and we fell asleep that first night
to the soothing sounds of rushing water coming out of the snow-
capped peaks that surround Estes Park.

There's a reason why people sell the sounds of nature on CD

and there's a reason why people buy them; the babbling brook that ran by our hotel room did wonders to ease our frayed nerves. We spent the next two days decompressing from the previous week. Rachel and I found fun things to do with Ben during the day and I was able to catch up on work with my laptop at night. The mountains and the scenery around us were so overwhelmingly beautiful that it took my mind away from the dark cloud on the horizon to the north. Literally, a dark cloud. The fire, the smoke, the media, the meetings, the frustration, and the tears...it had worn us out. No one sane could continue being sane under all that pressure. I had no interest in returning to Fort Collins any time soon.

I wanted to ride out the storm in Estes Park. I figured we could just stay in the mountains until the fire was contained and we would all be allowed to go home, assuming there was still a place we could still call home that wasn't ash and misery.

My family was doing really well and for the first time in more than a week, I wasn't stressed out of my mind. Unfortunately for me, all of that changed the next night at dinner.

It was supposed to be a family get-together. Rachel's parents had spent the last few days of the evacuation in Raymond with Rachel's aunt and collectively, we were really looking forward to sitting down and eating a meal together. We decided to meet up in Lyons, a small town at the edge of the mountains that is often referred to as the "gateway to the Rockies." David, Lisa, Rachel, Ben, and I convened at a brewpub in Lyons called Oskar Blues, known for their craft beers and BBQ. It was great to be together again.

It had only been a week, but considering the incredible amount of stress we were all under, and considering that we live together on the same piece of property and are used to seeing each other every day, a week is a long time to be apart. We caught up on the last few days and then sat down to order some food.

Moments later, David took out his phone and his face went ash white. I'll never forget what he said as long as I live.

"Looks like we lost it all, guys." He then read from his screen: "19595 Buckhorn Road: Structures on fire. All animals have been cleared out."

This is our physical address at Ohana—the physical address of the property before we divided it, but our address nonetheless. My heart sank to the bottom of the ocean.

The next few minutes are a blur to me now. Our food arrived, but I didn't taste a single bite of it as it slid down my throat into the black cauldron of despair formerly known as my stomach. Rachel and I were desperately trying to confirm or deny this devastating new piece of information with the data service on our cell phones while eating and also dealing with our son.

Ben was playing with a balloon the restaurant gave him and suddenly it got away from him. It floated into the sky and disappeared. He freaked out like he normally freaks out when he loses a balloon and we found ourselves trying to help him deal with his perceived loss while trying to deal with our own perceived loss.

It was this crazy parallel of possession and the sudden divorce of possession. Rachel took off to go find Ben another balloon and that left me wondering if philosophically, we had it all wrong. Maybe it was just a house and a bunch of stuff, and although it wouldn't be anywhere near as easy to replace as a helium-filled balloon, at the end of the day it was just material possessions that could be replaced.

Yes, technically, but at what a price? I thought of all the stress, aggravation, and backbreaking work that had gone into planning and building our two houses, let alone the vast amount of hard work that had gone into transforming Ohana in the past seven years. I couldn't even imagine doing it all over again.

Even if the insurance company cut us a check for our loss, there was no way that I was going to spend the next two to three years schlepping materials back and forth from Home Depot and arguing with subcontractors all over again. No way in hell. It was an unimaginable reality.

I figured that some of the victims of the fire would want to rebuild their homes and if we did in fact lose ours, I would ultimately have to make that decision, but felt 100 percent certain at the time that I could not put myself through it again.

The ominous message regarding our property going up in flames had been posted on Twitter, which I don't use and don't really know how to use. This only added to my frustration. I called a few of my friends to see if they could help us confirm or deny the statement but fifteen minutes later, with our whole family sitting there banging away on our phones, none of us had any new information that could determine whether the report about Ohana was true or false.

Rachel and I drove back to Estes Park shaking our heads the whole way. None of it made any sense. Each part of the statement could be dissected and logically challenged, but not entirely discredited.

"19595 Buckhorn Road"—why would someone describe our property using the old physical address and not Ohana Way? It could be that they had an older map or a GPS system that wasn't showing our recent minor land division.

"Structures on fire."—the most recent online fire maps didn't show the burn lines as having advanced any farther in the last couple of days, but what if the maps weren't showing the latest news? What if some of those embers jumped the road and now one or more of the homes on our property were on fire?

"All animals have been cleared out."—that didn't make any sense. There weren't any animals left on the property, at least not any animals that we knew of. Our cats and dogs came with us when we left, and the Humane Society had gotten behind the checkpoints earlier in the week and had cleared out all of our chickens. I was able to get through to them on the phone and they confirmed that they had not set up any sort of shelter on our property.

But, what if the fire crews had set up one of our barns as a temporary animal shelter sometime in the last week for animals evacuated from structures that were in imminent danger or on fire? It was an unlikely scenario, but it was still a possibility.

Each part of the report had a giant question mark over it. What if? I barely slept that night, or the next. I had horrible dreams of our beloved valley going up in flames. I spent every spare second over the next forty-eight hours researching the different segments of the ominous statement.

I know I wasn't the only one. David attempted to contact the person behind the Twitter post. The person initially replied, but after he searched David's full name online and figured out that David was an attorney, he stopped communicating.

I kept digging and found out that the person behind the report wasn't even in Colorado. The Tweet had been posted from somewhere in Virginia. Why would someone in Virginia be concerned with a disaster in Colorado and what business did this person have making statements about property on the other side of the country? The whole situation was infuriating.

In the end, we were 99 percent certain that the person behind the Tweet was just an opportunist with a police scanner, posting one alarming piece of information after another on various accidents and disasters around the country in an effort to get people to follow him on Twitter.

We reasoned that he had heard police chatter on a structure with animals in it behind the lines of the High Park Fire, Google'd "animal sanctuary" or "animal boarding," came across our old physical address (which used to be an animal sanctuary before we owned the property) and then took it upon himself to post an alarming update on Twitter in an effort to call attention to himself.

An update that he couldn't back up and an update he refused to confirm or deny when confronted by one of the owners of the property. Couldn't he have then posted a short statement explaining his actions to ease our troubled minds? It was such an aggravating situation.

I eventually turned my back on it, 99 percent certain that this guy was wrong, but still…one percent scared. I couldn't be 100 percent certain because I could not view Ohana with my own eyes to confirm or deny anything. Words cannot describe this frustration. It had been more than a week since I had seen our home and I began to realize how incredibly homesick I was, and how weary I had become with the evacuation and the uncertainty that came with it.

Strangers could post whatever they wanted about your property, whether it was true or not, and you had to just suck it up if they didn't respond to your pleas for more information.

Somehow, some way, on the tail of this circus, my family and I cleared out of Estes Park and found ourselves back in Fort Collins a few days later. We were right back in the thick of it.

SEVEN

Return to Ohana II: Electric Boogaloo

The scene had not improved in Fort Collins while we were gone—it had only gotten worse. The persistent hot weather and the lack of precipitation had hampered any efforts to control the High Park Fire and nearly two weeks into it, it was still zero percent contained. ZERO containment, which is a fancy way of saying absolutely out of control. The number of homes lost totaled more than 180 with no end in sight.

Rachel, Ben, and I temporarily moved back into the Secret Compass warehouse for the time being, until we could find something more permanent. I came back to a mountain of work that had accumulated over the time I had spent in Estes Park and I was really behind. I put my nose to the grindstone, pulling sixteen-hours days to get back on top of things at the shop.

In the meantime, the recent Twitter post about our property continued to haunt me. Like I said, I was 99 percent certain that Ohana was out of immediate danger, but still one percent uncertain and the fact that I missed being at home was really getting to me.

I wasn't sleeping well and after tossing and turning through a couple more sleepless nights, I got it in my head that I needed to go back and see Ohana for myself, once and for all.

Also, our garden had gone nearly two weeks without precipitation or watering and if somebody didn't get up there and do something, we would lose it for the season. Obviously, this was a small price to pay when more than 180 families had lost their homes and everything in them, but all the same, I couldn't imagine an empty harvest, especially if I was in even the slightest position to do something about it.

The gears began to turn in my mind. There was no way that I was going to get back home with a vehicle, that much was clear. My truck was stuck up at Ohana, but even if I borrowed my dad's truck, it wouldn't have made any difference. The National Guard was manning the barricades, and their checkpoint was farther up the canyon than the police checkpoint I had successfully circumvented two weeks prior.

There was no way that I or anyone else was going to get around the new blockade; the National Guard had seen to it when they set it up. Their checkpoint was at a particular place in the road where the natural terrain on either side of it was too steep to navigate, even if I went off-road. Off-road with a vehicle, that is.

I began plotting my second return to Ohana on a mountain bike. I tried emailing my friends Curt and Kelly, the couple that had lost their home in the Crystal Mountain Fire the year before. They had moved into a house farther down the canyon; it was behind the evacuation lines, but when they were supposed to evacuate like everyone else, they didn't leave.

Luckily, since they were still far enough from the actual burn zone, they still had electricity and that meant Internet access as well. I got an email back from Curt within the hour with detailed maps on the trails I could use to bypass the roadblock on a mountain bike. I grinned to myself. Having spent more than thirty years of his life living in the area, Curt knew the lay of the land more than anyone and he was willing to help.

I could rendezvous at his house before making the final push to Ohana. That was, assuming I could even get to his house. The National Guard barricade had a clear view down the canyon, and if they had anyone with binoculars, they'd literally see me coming from miles away.

I couldn't just drive up to within a couple hundred yards of their blockade and go peddling up into the hills. I'd have to start from a point much lower in the canyon and take the long way around the checkpoint. I would have to stay completely out of sight, on trails I had never ridden before, for what possibly could be hours on end, if I had any hope of getting past the National Guard.

I talked myself out of it and then back into it several times. Thankfully, my friends intervened.

I ran the whole plan by my employees, who also happen to be my good friends. I had just hired Andy, the man behind the songs for Peace Officer, in May. He had given me a shot to get back into music five years prior and we have been really good friends ever since. Andy was game.

He had a mountain bike and the skills to go along with it, but he wasn't keen on taking his $3,000 mountain bike into the unknown, where he might have to abandon it if anything went wrong. He talked me out of using mountain bikes altogether.

Andy reasoned that we could make better time if we hiked

in a straight line rather than zigzagging up and down trails we didn't know. Also, if we ran into any terrain that was too rough to handle on bikes, we wouldn't have to worry about hauling them with us or abandoning them.

If I haven't said it before, I'll say it now: my employees are really bright guys and I listen carefully to everything they say, whether it applies to the company, or my private life, or anything in between. Andy was 100 percent right. Especially sitting here in this chair, looking back on it all.

We spent the next hour organizing what would be a ten to twelve mile hike around the barricades. I reasoned that if we could get to Ohana by nightfall, and assuming that our houses hadn't burned down, we could spend a couple of hours there before driving back to town in my truck, which was still parked next to my dad's house.

I presumed that the National Guard wouldn't be concerned with vehicles *leaving* the burn area, and we wouldn't have any problems exiting at the barricades. We could be back in town by midnight.

Andy and I made a couple of stops to pick up food, water, and headlamps, and then had a friend drop us off at Bobcat Ridge, the trail system I had driven right through with my truck two weeks prior. It was about six to seven miles south of Curt's house. We started hiking at around 5:00 p.m.

Despite our late afternoon start, the sun was still blazing hot and I began to sweat profusely as Andy and I hiked our way up the mountains to the west of the county road. We figured that we would climb as far to the west as we could to avoid having anyone in the houses along the road spot us, or the National Guard, if they were scanning the horizon with binoculars.

The video camera I brought with me had an excellent zoom

lens on it and I used it from time to time to check in on the journey ahead and the barricades to the east of us.

The first part of the hike was reasonably easy and we made good time. Andy and I walked and talked, switching back and forth in conversation between the band and the company, to our families. I was grateful to have a friend keep me company. We were able to get around the National Guard blockade in a couple of hours and Curt's house was only a couple of miles away as the crow flies.

The problem was, we were having a hard time following a straight line. The gullies that drained water off the mountain we were hiking were getting wider and deeper, and consequently taking longer and longer to navigate.

Andy succeeded in putting his hand on a cactus and gashing up his legs; he was wearing shorts and with the bramble bush getting denser, it was taking us a lot of extra time to cover ground. We pressed on.

The last mile turned into two miles as we were forced to take extended detours around houses that were in the way. We couldn't be certain who had evacuated and who had stayed behind, and we didn't want to get into any confrontations. We knew we'd be seen as looters and if one of those residents popped out of one of the houses with a shotgun, we'd be sitting ducks. We went to great lengths to stay out of the line of sight.

The two of us got to a point where Curt's house was on the very next hill, only five hundred feet away, but yet almost impossibly out of reach. The terrain had saved the best for last. The final gully had Buckhorn Creek running through the bottom of it, and the creek had cut a path through the rock that seemed like it was thousands of feet below us. It was practically a cliff on one side and definitely a cliff on the other side.

Andy I spent almost an hour carefully scaling our way down into the creek bed, only to find that there was no way out. The towering wall of rock to the east offered no passage. Luckily, the stream had run nearly dry in the recent summer drought conditions so we were able to follow it upstream, walking right in the creek bed.

We kept going until we came to a pool of water that was a couple of feet deep and surrounded by a thick crop of poison ivy on either side. I was wearing long pants so I went first, in order to stamp out a trail for Andy to follow.

At that point, Andy and I separated. I had found a spot on the cliff wall that seemed like it was navigable, but Andy wasn't convinced. I was a third of the way up the cliff side before he told me he was going to keep hiking north to look for an easier spot to get out of the ravine. I was past the point of no return, as it would have been more dangerous to go back the way I came than to keep going, so I pressed on by myself, blindly putting one hand in front of the other in search of solid handholds.

Each step got me closer and closer to the top, but the farther I went, the more I started to freak out. I'm scared of heights and the view behind me was making me nauseous the higher I climbed. I was also terribly afraid of running into a rattlesnake or a hornet's nest or something else living along that cliff wall. What would I do, then? There would be no escape.

I was starting to seriously regret the route I had selected, but I didn't have a choice, I had to keep going. I gritted my teeth and pushed on. One hand after another, one hand after another. At one point, I stepped wrong and the boulder I was counting on to hold me suddenly shifted. I scrambled to regain a single handhold as the entire ledge I was standing on began to disintegrate.

Luckily, I secured myself by grabbing the roots of a small

tree that was growing out of the cliff side, right as the loose rock gave way and thundered into the gorge below me. I was glad that Andy had cut out on his own instead of following me up my route. He would've caught all that loose rock right in the face.

I shook my head. That's all we needed, a serious injury or a fatality in a place that no search and recovery team could ever reach, as if search and recovery was even available. I slowly pulled myself up using the tree as leverage. I prayed that it would hold my weight until I got a firmer grip on something else.

Once I found secure footholds, I took a minute to catch my breath and review the last few minutes. Unfortunately for me, it became a review of the last two weeks. I peered over the edge at the riverbed below me, thirty or forty feet down. The fall could kill a man. *What the hell are you doing, Cooper??*

I hadn't anticipated the kind of danger I was in before I started out on this journey. I stood there wondering if I would have even contemplated the hike I was on or if I would've done half the things I'd done in the past two weeks if I wasn't under such duress.

I'm just as capable as the next guy of making bad decisions, but I'd like to think I'm not prone to making them. I honestly think it was the prolonged exposure to such a high level of stress. Stress can make people do crazy things and there I was, right in the middle of a crazy thing.

Fortunately for me, I don't do much crying over spilled milk, and the reasons for my return to Ohana began to ring louder and louder in my head. I wiped the sweat off my brow and reached for the next handhold. Within a minute or so, I had pulled myself up onto another ledge and within another few minutes, I had reached the top of the cliff.

My clothes were full of thistles and I was exhausted, but

other than that, I was okay. I hiked for another thirty seconds or
so before I caught sight of my friend Curt standing at the edge
of his land, grinning down at me. His timing was perfect. Now all
we had to do was find Andy. I spent the next ten minutes walking up and down the cliff side, hollering my friend's name, but
to no avail. I was starting to get worried, as he wasn't answering.

Finally, after what seemed like eternity, Andy emerged from
the creek bed to the north of Curt's property. He had followed the
ravine until it gave way to a steep but navigable hillside. Mission
accomplished! We had successfully made it to the rendezvous
point in just under four hours.

I used Curt's phone to let my wife know that we were okay; I
had promised Rachel before I left that I would call once I got to
Curt's place and I followed through. Once I got off the phone,
Andy and I rewarded ourselves with a few beers as we discussed
the rest of the journey ahead of us.

There were still another three or four miles to go, up the
county road, to get to Ohana. Curt and Kelly tentatively offered
us one of their two cars, but the car they had to spare had a bad
battery in it and that meant we'd have to leave it running the
whole time we had it. I didn't know how much time I'd need once
I got home, so that didn't seem like a viable option.

Also, the road ahead of us would have official vehicles coming and going on it and that might spell trouble. The National
Guard and the local police were patrolling for looters and if we
got pulled over in someone else's car, we could get arrested and
then they'd tow that car. We couldn't risk losing Curt and Kelly's
vehicle or getting incarcerated.

Andy and I were ready to just keep hiking like we had been
for the last four hours, but then Curt came up with an alternate

plan. He had a couple of old mountain bikes that just needed to have their tires pumped up, and would we like to borrow those? We didn't need to be asked twice. We knew we could make fast work of the distance ahead of us if we could ride the county road all the way to Ohana on a couple of bikes. All we had to do was get off the pavement in a hurry if we heard any vehicles approaching, and considering that we were losing light fast, the cover of nightfall would work to our advantage. We took off just after dusk.

* * *

The first part of the ride was easy; it was a long downhill ride that wrapped around a few bends along the way. Andy and I coasted and peddled our way through a mile or so in a few minutes. We were beginning to make a push up one of the hills south of Ohana when a vehicle suddenly came up fast behind us. In a panic, we dragged the bikes off the pavement and flung ourselves behind a dumpster, just as a fire truck went roaring by. It was a really close call.

As we waited to make sure there were no additional vehicles accompanying the truck, I caught a whiff of the garbage brewing in that dumpster. God Almighty. It was the first clue of what was to come. Naturally, with the evacuation stretching more than two weeks, that also meant no services, including garbage trucks. I quickly realized how putrid all the garbage cans, dumpsters, refrigerators, and freezers were going to be once everyone got to go home. That was going to be a bad scene.

After making sure the coast was clear, Andy and I got back on the road. Not two minutes later we saw a set of oncoming headlights abruptly appear just ahead of us and had only a few seconds to get the bikes and ourselves out of sight. I literally threw my bike off the edge of the pavement and dove into the bushes. We waited awhile before continuing on, but I was really starting to get paranoid that we were going to get caught. I started riding with my head cocked to one side in an effort to try and hear oncoming vehicles before we saw them so we'd have a little time to react. Fortunately, we did not run into another vehicle until we were in the "narrows," the short, tight part of the canyon that sits just below Ohana. We saw and heard the last vehicle coming long before it was upon us and we were comfortably off the road when it passed.

My heart began to race as we closed in on the last three hundred feet before the entrance to our property. I didn't smell smoke, which was a good indicator that everything might be okay. We rounded the last curve and turned our bikes off the pavement onto the dirt driveway. We were home free.

Andy and I immediately hiked all the way up to my dad's house at the top of the mountain to get a better view of the burn line. I was relieved to see that fire had not come any closer to Ohana since the last time I had come home.

There was no sign of flame or fire anywhere to the immediate north or west of us. The horizon to the southwest of us was glowing orange, indicating that the fire had advanced into the hills behind High Park, but that was more than five miles away. Everything at Ohana was okay. I could finally confirm with my own two eyes, with 100 percent certainty, that there were no "structures on fire" on our property, as the jerk from Virginia had proclaimed in his Twitter post. What a relief.

I tried to open my dad's front door, with the intention of retrieving his laptop. It was locked. I ran around to the back door and tried that—same story. I had forgotten to pick up his keys before I left town and was now locked out of his house altogether, or so it seemed.

Suddenly, to my immediate right, I heard a high-pitched rattling somewhere in the darkness next to me. I jumped back five steps in a heartbeat and then quickly returned with my headlamp turned on. A small rattlesnake was coiled and ready to strike, just a few feet away.

Most people don't know this, but the juveniles are actually a lot more danger than the adults. The larger ones give you a warning shot of venom with their bite, but the smaller ones try and give you all the venom they are carrying, all in one strike.

I couldn't believe my eyes. We had just hiked six to seven miles, including a fifty to sixty foot blind climb up the side of a cliff without running into a single rattlesnake the entire time, only to find one right at my dad's doorstep.

I initially was going to let him go, but then realized he might set up shop in the rocks by my dad's door and bite my dad some day. I hunted around until I found a heavy rock and then executed the snake. Sorry reptile lovers, I'm not in the habit of killing things in nature, but I can't have my family in danger.

Anyway, after eliminating the threat, I shinnied up one of the poles holding up my dad's deck, in hopes that he had not locked his patio door before he left. I was in luck. I swung the door open and was immediately greeted with the overpowering odor coming from his refrigerator. It was overbearing, and the fridge's doors weren't even open.

Over two weeks without power and temperatures in the one hundreds had turned whatever was in his fridge into something evil. I held my breath as I watered my dad's plants with one of the water bottles sitting on his counter and then retrieved his laptop. I couldn't wait to get out of there.

I fired up my truck and drove it down to my place. Stepping into my house was like taking a step into another dimension. It was such a crazy experience. I've often tried to put my feelings into words when reflecting back on this day during the evacuation and I have never felt that I properly expressed myself. I'll try and get it right here.

* * *

It was clear that the fire department had paid our home a visit while we were gone. The handle on the front door of the house had been wrapped up with some kind of caution tape, which put me on edge just at the sight of it. It was an eerie foreshadowing of what was to come.

With power out on the entire ranch, Andy and I had to turn on our headlamps to enter the house. We pushed our way through the front door into the great room. The stench coming from the kitchen was unbearable.

After making a grand seafood dinner for myself on that last night I was at home, I had just piled all the dishes and pans into the sink without even considering how long I might be gone. I was so out of it when I left, it simply never occurred to me that I should've been preparing for what could be a lengthy evacuation.

In our extended absence, the dishes and the debris on them transformed into something unholy. The garbage can beneath the sink, which was topped off with shrimp skins and clam shells, had spent the last two weeks conspiring to redefine the word *putrid* to the English speaking people of planet Earth. It was such a wretched assault on the senses.

I held my breath and reached for the faucet on the kitchen sink, fully intending to power through the nausea and get all the dishes cleaned up. Much to my surprise, when I pulled the handle on the faucet, nothing came out of the tap. No water. I stared at the tap in disbelief.

I knew that with the power out, the booster pump in my basement wouldn't turn on so we'd have low pressure, but even with low pressure, we should have still had gravity-fed water from the cistern farther up the mountain. There should've been close to 2,000 gallons still sitting in there, even after watering the garden the last time I was at home. It didn't make sense.

I ran out to my truck and drove back up the driveway to my dad's place to check out the cistern. I anxiously spun the top off the hatch and peered into the cement vault with my headlamp. Much to my chagrin, it was bone dry. Somehow, some way, nearly 2000 gallons of water had simply vanished.

There didn't appear to be any water anywhere on the ranch, and since the pumps in the wells couldn't run without power, there was no way to replenish water any time soon.

My heart sank. I was really hoping to be able to water the garden while I was home—it was one of the main reasons I had spent the last five hours trekking around the river and through the woods, to get back to Ohana. I felt completely defeated as I returned to my house.

The stench from the kitchen wasn't even registering anymore as I struggled to come to terms with the overwhelming reality of the moment. I couldn't quite place it at first, but it slowly came to me. *I felt like a stranger in my own house.*

It had been more than two weeks since I had been home and during that extended time period, in the flurry of trying to be the best husband, dad, son, son-in-law, friend, and manager I could be, while under serious duress, I could no longer recall the nuances that defined comfort within my personal space, where I lived.

I couldn't remember how the towel on the floor outside the bathroom got there, or how the cup with a rotting tea bag in it got onto the coffee table. I couldn't readily recall why there was a set of pliers on the banister, or what my son was doing with a stack of nickels in his bathroom.

Throughout the entire house, I ran into one mystery after another—trivial details from everyday life that had transformed into affirmations that I was no longer familiar with my own home. My short-term memory had filled up with a substitution of my everyday life rather than my actual life.

Looking back on it all, I suspect that all of this was amplified by the fact that I couldn't turn on any of the lights in my house. With the power out, I was seeing my house for the first time in two weeks through the narrow view of a headlamp, a battery-powered LED bulb fastened to an elastic cord mounted just above my eyes.

The rooms in our house came alive as sweeping triangles of bright light and then darkness, like scenes out of the underwater documentaries done on the *Titanic*, resting two miles down in the Atlantic Ocean.

I literally felt like I was some kind of a ghost in an underwater grave being given a tour through a museum of what used to be my home, a hundred years after some cataclysmic event. It was such a surreal experience that it was making me uncomfortable— I didn't want to stay any longer than I had to.

I made my way to the camping supplies in the basement, where I knew I had a jug with at least three gallons of water in it. I used it to water all the plants in the house and then gathered some extra clothes before clearing out. It really bothered me that I was relieved to be leaving my own home, but there wasn't anything I could do to make myself feel better.

David and Lisa's house felt like a tomb, too. I made the

mistake of opening their drink fridge in the garage, the one that wasn't hooked up to their generator. Someone had put a basket of strawberries in there along with the sodas and two weeks later, that little basket of strawberries took up an entire shelf in the fridge. It nearly turned my stomach inside out.

I went through their house with the water jug and watered all their plants. I moved from room to room with my headlamp guiding the way, feeling very much like I was in a haunted house.

I could almost feel the energy in the dining room, emanating from the table that we had sat around so many times as a family. The memories of joy and laughter drifted through my head like voices from a dream long forgotten. It conjured up such powerful feelings of homesickness that I just wanted to just lie down on the floor underneath the table and go to sleep.

I made myself keep moving. I came to the last plant and poured the last of the water out of the jug. Now, all I had to do was come up with a way to refill that jug thirty or forty times and I'd get the whole garden squared away.

In between the nagging questions that surrounded our empty cistern, it dawned on me that there might still be water in the lake. I wasn't sure how much the firefighters had drained in their efforts to put out the fire on the mountain across from Ohana, but they couldn't have drained every last drop.

Andy and I would have to wade through the mud, but if there was any water left, we could do runs to and from the lake with buckets and transport them with my truck. It would be a lot of work, but we'd get the whole garden watered.

I was stacking buckets in the back of my truck when it came to me...the smaller cistern. There are two wells and two cisterns on the property, but we rarely use the deep well. I don't believe it was even in use at the time of the evacuation.

The main cistern up on the mountain by my dad's place was empty, but the smaller one located in the pump house for the deep well might still have water in it. This pump house was only fifty feet from the garden. I threw open the door and peered inside. Lo and behold, the smaller cistern was full of water. I spun the lid off and found that a five-gallon bucket could easily pass through the neck at the top of the cistern.

Andy and I began filling buckets and running them to and from the garden two at a time. I checked the greenhouse first and was surprised to find that even having gone more than two weeks in the blazing heat without water, the tomato plants were in relatively good shape. They were a little wilted, but very much alive. It was the same thing with just about everything else, including the peppers and eggplants. There were only a couple of things that looked like they were past the point of recovery.

I heavily watered everything in the greenhouse and then turned my attention to the basil and the greens in the garden. I must have made thirty trips with a bucket in each hand to and from the pump house before the conditions made it too hard to keep going.

My clothes were thoroughly soaked from head to toe and I smelled like a sack of garbage. I was sweating so hard that my headlamp kept slipping off my head, and I had already fallen down twice in the darkness. We were just too tired to continue and decided to call it quits.

We had heavily watered more than two-thirds of the garden by hand and the most important things now had a fighting chance to go at least another week or so without getting into trouble. If only we could get some damn rain.

It was close to midnight and both Andy and I were completely exhausted. We loaded the bikes we had borrowed into the back of the truck and cleared out. After dropping off the bikes at Curt's place, we drove down the mountain to the National Guard blockade.

On the way, Andy and I concocted a fictitious excuse for why we had waited so long to evacuate from "our" property. I was prepared to get pulled over and possibly questioned, but when we pulled up to the lights, the guards on duty just waved us through.

EIGHT

Mordor

I t had been more than two weeks since the mandatory evacuation was ordered and by the third week in June, the High Park Fire was only 10 percent contained. Due to the persistent hot weather, high winds, and lack of precipitation, the southern rim was the only border the firefighters had managed to contain. Everything to the northeast and northwest was still raging out of control.

Larimer County had not seen a drop of rain in weeks, nor had the rest of Colorado. Our entire state was a giant tinderbox waiting to ignite. It didn't take long.

On June 24th, a fire that started in a canyon northwest of Colorado Springs quickly spiraled out of control and came right into the city. Driven by high winds, the Waldo Canyon Fire annihilated entire neighborhoods as it expanded. The houses in the way didn't even have time to catch fire and burn to the ground— they simply exploded into giant fireballs at the blink of an eye due to the intense heat. I stared at videos that people had posted online in total disbelief.

It didn't stop there. Within the span of a few days, there were a total of *fourteen* different wildfires burning out of control across the state of Colorado, including one in Estes Park where Rachel and I had gone to escape the stress and tension in our own city.

The state's resources, even with federal and international assistance, were spread razor thin. There were simply not enough firefighters or equipment to combat all of these wildfires at once.

I remember seeing a photo someone had doctored and put up on Facebook showing one of the "Welcome To Colorful Colorado" entrance signs you see on the interstate when you cross state lines, set to a backdrop of Mordor, from *The Lord of the Rings*. It made me so sad. I was shocked at what was happening to our beautiful state, our home.

Two plus weeks into our own evacuation, with half the state on fire and no end in sight, I was finding it harder and harder to cope. The strain of living day to day in the Secret Compass warehouse with my wife and son, while trying to run a business with three employees and all of the stress that comes with it, at the same time, in the same place, was becoming unbearable. I was losing it. Again.

My wife was working hard to find an apartment for our family and my dad to stay in, and despite the high demand for temporary housing, she pulled it off. We had a place to go. The problem was, on the evening we were supposed to move into the new apartment, I fell apart.

I was up to my eyeballs in work for Secret Compass, covering for two employees that were out plus struggling with two major credit card charge-backs filed against the company that amounted to thousands.

Rachel and I had plans to meet up with some friends for dinner and then move our stuff to the new apartment, but I never made it. Rachel and I ended up in a major fight. F bombs were dropped and all of a sudden, I found myself sleeping alone on the couch in the warehouse without my wife and son. *Wonderful job, Cooper. Couldn't hold it together for another couple of hours.*

This was the beginning of a very difficult time for me, as I struggled to cope with not only the ongoing stress and pressure of life as an evacuee, but also the added strain of having to do it alone. The weight of the last couple of weeks came down on me full force.

Without Rachel and Ben, I desperately tried to fill the void in my life with work. The summer months of June, July, and August demand an enormous amount of time and energy of anyone trying to make a living in the limited edition collectibles world, as the manufacturers traditionally debut their new merchandise lines at Comic Con in San Diego.

This convention usually takes place in late July every year and the dealers work late into the night to get the new listings and promotional work ready to go. It all starts about a month before the event, in late June. I put in some long hours over the next couple of days trying to take my mind off the situation with my wife. Eighteen-hour days, back to back.

· I struggled to resolve the two credit card charge-backs and late one night, I eventually succeeded in clearing the last of the two, but had no one to share my moment of triumph with. I went out the next night and got totally drunk with some friends, but in the morning the stress was waiting right there for me and all the alcohol in the world couldn't fill the void in my life.

When I was young and single, relationships didn't carry as much weight with me—I was used to being alone when I wasn't in the company of friends. I wasn't dependent on anyone, but the loneliness was hard to bear, particularly in the later years. I yearned for companionship, especially when I stopped making music full time, and I was really happy to be getting out of the fast lane when I met Rachel.

At the same time, when you've been married for years and years, your happiness is intertwined with your spouse's happiness and it's really hard to be happy when you're not getting along. You're sharing your life with someone, and when that someone isn't there, you miss them terribly.

The longer the deadlock went, the worse I felt. The walls seemed to be caving in on all sides. I slipped into a jagged depression that bounced back and forth between being frustrated with myself for not being able to cope and feeling guilty that my wife was having to deal with the circumstances of our ordeal alone, since I was too proud to admit that my inability to cope was to blame.

This was all intertwined with a deep-seated resentment I've harbored for years over the relentless workload I've shouldered to see my company succeed. It has made me schizoid, to some degree. I'm a crazy, driven bastard that wants the financial security for my family and my crew so that no one has to go without. Yet, at the same time, when I see someone riding their skateboard down the sidewalk or floating down the river with a beer in their hand, I wonder what the hell happened and how I wound up working twelve hours a day, for years on end.

The complete lack of free time has simultaneously given me security and hobbled me. I normally do a good job of suppressing this conflict, but occasionally, when I'm having a hard time, it forces its way to the surface.

To make matters worse, one night while going through my

voicemail, I came across a message from none other than Ben, my three-year-old son, telling me that he missed me and wished I would come "home." I wanted to throw myself off the nearest bridge.

I tossed and turned for the rest of the night, praying that the monster beneath the trap door would continue to lie dormant. I was already worn down from the evacuation and the fight and I didn't have the energy to swim up to clarity, so I sank to the bottom.

Being slave to such a demanding schedule, despite the benefits of security, has its costs. Time. Tick Tock. Time is sliding by, and all the people and places that I love and cherish are slipping into the sands of time. Tick Tock. I want to stop the clock, hit pause, time out…I need to spend a lot more time with my mom before she's gone. And my dad. And all my friends. Tick Tock.

I subconsciously walk on pins and needles every day of my life hoping that I can stave off the inevitable for just another day. The quicksands of time—slowly pulling everything I hold precious into eternal darkness. I dream of creating a thousand clones, and blasting them all into the universe, to experience the warmth and love of all my friends and family before they pass; all that I cannot do as a single stream of consciousness, in a single lifetime.

The desperation burning like fire, flowing like a river of magma just beneath the surface. Desperation that I cannot show in my everyday life for fear that the people around me perceive it as weakness. Yet, it is most definitely there, every second of every waking hour.

At my age, some men yearn for cars they have never possessed, women they could not seduce, and wealth they could not earn. My mid-life crisis…being so busy that I do not have the time to spare, to spend with my loved ones. All of them, all at once.

NINE

Winding Down

I came to the surface a few days later and called my wife to apologize. She's a really good person, and thankfully, she let me back in. I had definitely not earned my readmission, but somehow I got another chance to prove that I was worth something. I could see in Rachel's eyes that my absence had deeply hurt her and everything wasn't going to be cool right away, but I was determined to pull it all back together.

I did my best to stabilize the situation. I shopped for groceries, made meals, and kept Ben occupied so Rachel could resume something that resembled a normal social life. We were in the third week of the evacuation and despite our efforts to create a sense of normalcy, neither of us could deny the reality of the situation.

We were both hopelessly worn down from the anxiety and stress of the situation. The High Park Fire continued to burn out of control to the north and northeast of Ohana.

The shocking news came one night as Rachel and I were monitoring the burn maps on our laptops: another fifty homes in the Glacier View subdivision had been lost in a single day. The mountain communities in Poudre Canyon were in imminent danger and more evacuations were being ordered by the hour. There didn't seem to be an end in sight—248 homes lost and counting.

Rachel and I did our best to distract ourselves. We met up with people from our community that were going through the same experience we were going through, and some of them had seen far worse.

One couple had spent two weeks trying to get behind the lines to check on their house, and when they finally made it back, there was simply nothing there. Their home and tool shed had been completely consumed by the fire, and the high winds had already dispersed the ash and debris in their absence. They didn't even get a chance to sift through the remains of what they owned. By the time they got behind the lines, everything they had left behind was just gone. The concrete foundations were the only telltale evidence that anything had ever been built there in the first place.

All the same, this couple was in high spirits and so were many of our other friends and neighbors, even people who had also lost their homes. Many people were determined to stay and help rebuild the community once we all got to go home. Rachel and I were invigorated by the optimism surrounding us and we were determined to see the evacuation through.

Despite not having decent clothes, we attended a wedding later that week that some friends of ours had invited us to. We wore some of the same clothes we had been wearing for the past three weeks, but we didn't let that bother us. It was a chance to blow off some steam and the two of us had a blast catching up with everyone.

My dear old friend Chris surfaced that week as well. He was taking part in a work-related convention and when the convention drew to a close, despite the fact that he knew I was out of house and home, he made a beeline straight for Colorado. I can't tell you how grateful I am to not only have good friends in my life, but to have them care about me in my time of need.

Another mutual friend put together a fun night down in Denver, and all of a sudden, the three of us were sitting in camping chairs, drinking beers, awaiting a show at Red Rocks Amphitheater. If someone would've told me that while being evacuated from my home, three weeks into it, I'd have a chance to sit there and get loaded with Jeff Heagerty and Chris Kurtz, two of my childhood friends, I wouldn't have believed it.

I needed a night like that so bad, I tell you. It seems like something so routine—a night out with your friends—until you find yourself under tremendous pressure due to a life-changing event, and then it's all you hope for. It's like finding water in the desert. It was such a relief, just to simply be distracted for a few hours, let alone to be distracted by two old friends and all the laughs that came with it.

Chris and I went back to Fort Collins the next day, and Chris would go on to spend the next week sleeping on the couch in the apartment Rachel, Ben, and I were sharing with my dad. I think it's fair to say that Chris brought a healthy dose of distraction to *all* of us; he breathed new life into what had been a tense situation for weeks on end.

The nights spent in front of laptops with our retinas burning out of our skulls gave way to dinners, drinks, reminiscing, and laughs. In the meantime, distracted from the stress that had permeated our lives for so long, we didn't take notice that the firefighters had turned the corner and all of a sudden, they were winning the war.

The containment percentage gradually moved up to 30, and then 40, and then 50. Then, a couple of days later, my cell phone rang and I heard that voice—the female computer-generated voice that sounded like it came from *Aliens*—emotionlessly informing me that the evacuation had been lifted in my area and that I could proceed home with caution.

I was in the Secret Compass warehouse when I got the call and it caught me by total surprise. After completely flipping out, I called Rachel to give her the good news. The two of us immediately set a plan into motion for how we would gather up our belongings, spread between the warehouse and the apartment, and finally go home.

Chris helped us pack up our son, our cat, our computers, our photos albums, and our clothes into three vehicles, and all of a sudden, the nightmare was over. We were going home.

* * *

I had a lot to think about on the drive back to Ohana. It's kind of like that point at the end of a blow-out fight with your girlfriend where everything is returning to normal, but deep down inside you know that you said and did things that you regret, that are probably not going to fly next time around. It's that tipping point where you realize that everything is going to be okay, yet you wish you had the chance to do it all over again, knowing in advance that everything is going to be okay.

The last three weeks flashed through my mind as I rounded corner after corner on the all-too-familiar drive home. Part of me was really down on myself. I was disappointed at the way I had handled various aspects of the evacuation, and frustrated at the way I had dropped the ball on communicating with people around me, particularly the people closest to me. My family deserves better. I'm sorry, Rachel.

Like I said, though, I don't spend much time crying over spilled milk, and as I glided into the last few bends on the county road before I hit Ohana, I came to terms with it all. My friends and family know me...I go ballistic when I'm cornered, but this is nothing new to them. They know me to be an extremely passionate person and unfortunately, I can't always control the energy that feeds my intense appetite for life, as much as I'd like to. There is a dark side of it and anyone who knows me, knows that I've worked hard to manage it.

Being a crazy, driven lunatic has brought many good things to my life, and despite all of the things that I regret or wish that I had done better, I can't deny that my personality has done more good than bad in the years I've been alive.

And, when it comes to the bad, I can make a thousand excuses, or I can just man up and say that I will try and come back stronger next time. In the true words of one of my earliest influences, written down once many years ago and repeated many times since then... "Try Again."

Epilogue

This story wouldn't be complete if I left everyone hanging, not only on the small mysteries created here and there within these pages, but also on the overall aftermath of the High Park Fire and its impact on our community.

Needless to say, after the three-week evacuation, it was so good to be home. Many people came back to nothing more than the charred remains of their houses and their belongings, and everyone at Ohana felt incredibly fortunate to have dodged not only one, but two fires in the previous two years (see photo 5). It felt like we were experiencing a miracle.

Despite our proximity to the High Park Fire, none of the structures on our property were affected. We didn't even have smoke damage, which apparently affected nearly everyone else. Many of our neighbors were unable to return to their homes due to smoke damage, which took weeks and months to resolve.

Ohana came through virtually unscathed. Well, almost. We came home to science experiments, formerly known as our refrigerators, in most of the structures. The airborne spores generated by food in an advanced state of decay can be really dangerous to human health, particularly for the young and the old, so I made sure that neither my dad nor my son were anywhere near the refrigerators when I cleaned them out.

Fortunately for all of us, the power had been turned back on at Ohana two days before we got to go home, so all of the rotten food in the freezers simply refroze. That at least kept the most revolting of the odors from overwhelming me. I still went above and beyond by donning not only a full-face respirator, but also a full biohazard body suit and gloves, to clear out the refrigerators.

David had the foresight to pick all of this equipment up at Home Depot on the way home, so I went into the job feeling protected from what was awaiting me. The problem was, even after clearing out all the rotten food, the fridges still smelled like something had died in them. Rachel and I removed every portable shelf and part and carefully cleaned each one with a combination of cleaners and baking soda. We scrubbed the insides over and over again.

Day by day, the odor gradually dissipated, and in time all of the refrigerators returned to normal working order. Our insurance company would have provided for new appliances if we insisted, but why dump perfectly good appliances into the landfill if all they needed was a little elbow grease and some perseverance?

* * *

Many people have asked me how it went with our insurance company once we got home. There is a knee jerk reaction in our society to always assume that the insurance company is trying to pull a fast one on the homeowner, but I can honestly say that we didn't have a bad experience.

I can't say that I agreed with every policy our particular insurance company had in place for our kind of emergency, but the claims adjustors that promptly appeared within a few days of our return to Ohana were fair and more importantly, they were human. They weren't the robots one expects in situations like this, reading from their policy books like automatons. The adjustors were sympathetic toward our ordeal and advised us on how we could maximize our claims as we completed the paperwork. Our out-of-pocket expenses were covered, for the most part, and we came away from the experience feeling that we had been treated fairly.

* * *

The mystery of the missing two thousand gallons of water from our main cistern was solved within a couple of days of our return to Ohana, but even after we found the leak, it was only the beginning of what would end up being a complicated problem relating to the fire and the drought conditions experienced that summer.

I traced the leak to a hose in the control pit and replaced it with a new hose, but even after the repair, we still couldn't get the main cistern to fill back up again. To make a long story short, both wells on the property were failing due to mechanical issues as well as the low water table.

I believe that the intermittent powering down and powering back up of the electrical service during the evacuation adversely affected the electrical components on both pumps, but considering that both pumps were nearly twenty years old, I went ahead and replaced both of them, along with new electronic sensors designed to protect the new equipment if the wells ran dry.

Unfortunately for us, while that did resolve the mechanical issues, the new equipment still couldn't bring back the water table. By the time we got to August, the water table was so low that one of the wells actually went dry. We got through the rest of the month on the deep well plus a few water deliveries from town that were pumped straight into the cistern. The early season snowstorms in the mountains above us got everything back to normal in September.

* * *

The garden...what a great story. The two returns to Ohana that I made during the evacuation kept just about everything from dying, but ultimately, since we didn't get a drop of rain in three weeks, I'm not sure that the garden would have survived on two single watering sessions alone—particularly because there were sections I simply did not have time to water, which had gone without for three weeks during a heat wave that saw one hundred-plus temperatures for days on end.

Much to our surprise, we got help from the last thing in the world we would have ever had expected to get help from: the weeds. We thought we'd be coming home to a barren wasteland, and the jungle awaiting us was a complete shocker.

One weed in particular went above and beyond, despite the lack of moisture, and it grew so thick and so tall that it actually shielded the lettuce, spinach, and other leafy greens from being dried out by the sun. Nearly everything we had planted survived, thanks to these weeds.

We were overwhelmed at first, dealing with how much work had to be done in the garden to bring it back up to speed, but then Rachel put a post up on Facebook and all of a sudden we had fifteen friends appear out of nowhere on a Saturday morning.

Within a few hours, the garden was back to normal. We are really grateful to everyone who showed up that day. Thanks again for your amazing support of Ohana and our family!

* * *

The yoga retreat…what unfortunate timing to have planned a retreat at Ohana. The three-week evacuation from the High Park Fire turned out to be the exact three weeks we had set aside for the yoga retreat. The entire group had to leave just two days into the session, and then could only return at the end of June—right as the session was scheduled to have come to a close.

After getting bounced around a couple times during that first week, the group finally found a permanent place to stay at a ranch just outside Loveland. The fire never advanced in that direction so they didn't have to worry about having to move again while they continued with the three-week course. Despite the major upheaval, the group did complete the course on time.

We met with a few of the original guests at Ohana on the day everyone was allowed to return home in our area and we did have a chance to say goodbye to some of our guests as they retrieved their belongings. Hopefully, the next time we attempt to share our property with friends and family, we won't be faced with having to evacuate our guests.

* * *

Curt and Kelly have begun construction of their new house, going up on the same concrete pad originally poured for their old house, which was destroyed by the Crystal Mountain Fire in 2011. I just spoke with Curt for the first time this summer, while reviewing final edits for this book. Curt bought a used sawmill earlier in the year and after cutting down most of the burned trees on his property, he is using the sawmill to turn what is left of the trees into the trusses and lumber they need for their new house. Apparently, the heat from the fire created "better than kiln-dried" lumber. It's an amazing story, which was just covered by North

Forty News, one of our local newspapers. It will be a glorious day when Curt and Kelly move into their new house, built from the trees salvaged from the fire that took their first house.

* * *

Dan the Digger did *not* lose his cabin in Rist Canyon, as was previously assumed. The fire ravaged the area where he lives and he did lose his shed, but not his cabin. Last I heard, he was hard at work rebuilding the shed...

* * *

As for me...I've often been asked, in the last year, how I am doing. The truth is, I am doing better. This book, like many of the lyrics I wrote in yesteryear, has been part of the healing process that I go through when I deal with adverse things that happen in my life. I'm still facing challenges when it comes to managing my time, but I am definitely paying more attention to my own limitations in terms of work and stress. That's good news for everyone around me. Looking back on everything I have written here, I clearly wish I had been better prepared for the evacuations. If I had one piece of advice to pass on to anyone who builds or buys a home: be 100% certain that your home, grounds, and your belongings are fully insured, for the complete cost of replacement. This changes often, as market conditions will continually drive up the costs of what your possessions will cost to replace them. It's easy to get complacent in life and then get caught being under-insured, when it's time to evacuate. Then, it's too late. You can skip a lot of heartache by staying diligent on your insurance policies. Of course, no evacuation will ever be easy, but if I had known then what I know now, I wouldn't have gotten so stressed out and I wouldn't have made so many mistakes.

* * *

In the past year, many people have asked me if our community could or would ever recover from such a catastrophic loss. The High Park fire scorched 259 homes and more than 137 square miles before it was fully contained. Could or would the mountain folk ever be able to make a comeback?

The answer is a resounding yes, and the healing began almost immediately after we got home. We got our first major downpour a week later. It rained for hours and hours on end, and the creeks roared with black water. Our lake came back in its entirety, thanks to this storm.

In July, the Forest Service began work on a massive project that provided runoff prevention and reseeding with hundreds of airdrops from helicopters over the burn areas. The annual Rist Canyon Volunteer Fire Department Labor Day Mountain Festival which draws thousands of people, came and went with heavier-than-usual support from Northern Colorado and beyond.

The Stove Prairie Elementary School reopened on schedule in September, right on cue. I remember thinking that with all of the homes that had burned down, there'd simply be no families left in the mountains and thus no kids left to attend the school. I pictured my son and a handful of other kids sitting in empty classrooms, but I underestimated the power and will of the community. Despite a few empty chairs here and there, the school and its students came back in full force for the 2012/2013 year.

I don't know the statistics on how many families have decided to rebuild homes that were lost, but for the ones that did, there is an extensive network available to them. Many compassionate people along the Front Range have volunteered their knowledge, their time, and their physical labor, for free, to help families that are determined to rebuild.

Many of the local businesses, including the big box stores,

have offered substantial discounts to residents specifically affected by the High Park Fire.

In summary, our mountain community is rebounding. The scars will take a long time to heal, but in time, they will heal and we will come back stronger. The trees will eventually grow back, and the people affected will either rebuild or relocate. The earth and the human race have both seen disasters far worse than ours…time and energy have healed them all.

Acknowledgments

My deepest condolences to the victims of the Black Forest Fire, the West Fork fire, and the families of the nine hotshot firefighters that died while battling a blaze in Arizona, all which took place while this book was being edited.

Thanks to Jerry, Anna, Rachel, Ben, David, Lisa, Tomas, PT, HC, PO, Allen, Andy, Erwin, Brad, Rys, Chris, Jeff, LaVonne of PixyJack Press, Mira, Diane, Eric Grosshans for his relentless support during editing, Alexa, Jen, Linda, Jerbear, everyone who opened their homes to us, the Rist Canyon Volunteer Fire Department and all of the firefighters, everywhere, for doing what you do.

Special thanks to you for buying this book, as part of the proceeds will go to the RCVFD!

The Author

J.S. Cooper is a writer and vocalist who first emerged with HeadCrash, an international recording group that helped define the fusion of social consciousness and alternative music in the 1990s. Since then, he has contributed to more than a dozen bands and publications. J.S. Cooper was clearly put on this Earth to reflect on the human condition. Despite the trauma experienced within these pages, he continues to live on a remote homestead known as "Ohana," west of Fort Collins, Colorado with his wife, his son, and their extended family.

www.evacueebook.com